Transformed to Transform

A Journey to Bring Change to a Community

Dr Modupe Omideyi

Scripture quotations taken from:

The Holy Bible, New International Version, Copyright © 1973, 1978, 1984 by International Bible Society.

The Amplified® Bible (AMPC),
Copyright © 1954, 1958, 1962, 1964, 1965, 1987 by The Lockman Foundation
Used by permission: www.Lockman.org

ISBN 978-1-907929-80-9

www.transformedtotransform.uk

Love and Joy Ministries Ltd
Liverpool Lighthouse
Oakfield Road
Anfield
L4 0UF

Cover design by Graeme Moodie

Editing and layout by Life Publications
www.lifepublications.org.uk

To our Lord and Saviour, Jesus Christ

Acknowledgements

I would like to thank all those who allowed me to interview them and include their stories in this book.

Thanks to Tani, who suggested the title and the original chapter outline for the book. He let me pin him down and interview him, and entrusted me with the rest.

I am indebted to Rev Dave Cave and Rev John Cavanagh for filling me in on the history of the development of the unity movement among the evangelical churches on Merseyside.

I would like to thank all those we have worked with, and who have supported us and partnered with us down through the years, including those in the city council and in our communities, our MPs and councillors.

Thanks to the many churches, friends and ministers, great men and women of God, who have prayed for, supported, worked with and encouraged us so faithfully. Thanks also to those who believed in what we were doing and have given their time and skills freely as trustees, advisers and volunteers.

Most particular and grateful thanks go to John and Rose Lancaster, who through their Foundation have given us support without which the ministries could not exist today.

I am grateful to those who gave encouraging and helpful feedback on the manuscript, providing the impetus for me to complete it.

Thank you, Tolu, Ibbie and Ladun, for encouraging me to start the book, and cheering me on till I finished it.

The best and greatest thanks of all go to God. I trust that his will in having this book written will be fully accomplished.

Commendations

This gripping narrative tells in unvarnished terms how two people dared to trust God and how God enabled them to make decisions and to act on them in faith. This transformative story illustrates God's providence that meets the needs of God's servants and helps them to become channels of blessings to others. This story about Pastors Tani and Modupe Omideyi is timely. It shows how God's servants can encourage people of different national, cultural and language backgrounds to gather together under a single roof for worship, learning, service, and mutual edification. Their ministry radiates a living faith in a living God. This story will certainly move the readers to reflect on their own faith journey and to undertake initiatives to worship God afresh, read God's Word, and to serve God's people first in their vicinity and then with others near and far.

Professor Daniel Jeyaraj,
Director of Andrew Walls Centre for the Study of African and
Asian Christianity, Liverpool Hope University

Tani and Modupe Omideyi are two of my heroes in the faith and it's a privilege to call them my friends. I tell their story and the story of Love and Joy Ministries whenever I get the chance. So, now you get an opportunity to read it first hand and to celebrate their amazing journey of obedience and faith.

From humble beginnings, squeezed into a rented flat in Toxteth, the church has grown into its present home in a refurbished cinema just a few hundred yards from Anfield Stadium, with a multitude of social and educational projects serving the community God has called them to.

Steve Clifford, General Director, Evangelical Alliance UK

To write a commendation for a book that I am part of the history of, brings me a lot of joy. I'm so proud that Pastors Modupe and Tani, who are both my spiritual mum and dad over the years, have catalogued their journey and stories as a means of encouragement and inspiration for emerging pioneers.

Their lives as exemplary can be seen throughout the book. Their faith, sacrifice, love, commitment to God and ministry and their determination to break barriers and open new frontiers despite limited resources and difficult circumstances are seen in every page of this book.

Their story and narrative are exemplary of anyone hoping to lead a church, ministry or mission that is not ethnic specific but embraces authentic relationship and service to anyone irrespective of race, colour, creed or social status.

I recommend this book for emerging leaders who are keen to learn from the elders, to the emerged leaders who are hoping to create a new narrative and to anyone who is keen to learn humility in service, sacrifice to calling and unshakeable faith in God.

Rev Canon Yemi Adedeji,
Director, One People Commission,
Evangelical Alliance UK

I much enjoyed the book and the story of Christian obedience being worked out over many years. What struck me most was how a long term commitment necessarily involves the whole family and that involves risk to the whole family. Entrusting your children to God is much harder than taking personal risks and Christian obedience is in truth a whole life commitment. That is the power of this story.

Sir Mark Hedley DL, retired High Court Judge;
Diocesan Chancellor, Liverpool

Commendations

I read the history of the whole Love and Joy story with fascination, but I also found the book personally very challenging. Their prayerfulness, obedience, commitment and hard grind were humbling.

Erica, Lady Hedley, Vice Chair of Governors,
The Academy of St Francis of Assisi, Liverpool

Transformed to Transform is a book filled with faith and is very inspirational. I am sure that many people will be encouraged and challenged to step out in faith too through reading it.

Lesley Sutton, Director, PassionArt

Transformed to Transform

Foreword

The mistake that many make about the episode when Jesus overturns the tables of the money-lenders in the Temple is to think that it is just a story about Jesus condemning corrupt business. But what we overlook is where the money-lenders were operating. They had been given the area of the Temple that was set aside for foreigners, races other than the Jewish people, to draw near to God. By filling this Court of the Gentiles with market stalls they were depriving the other races of their sacred space to come close to God.

Jesus stops the trading and stops any one walking though so he can restore the sacred space to the non-Jewish pilgrims to worship God. As he does so he quotes from the Prophet Isaiah that God's House should be a House of Prayer for all races. It is the fulfilling of a prophetic vision that God's Kingdom will be made up of people from all races and backgrounds. He is a God without frontiers.

The reason I start with this is because my abiding impression of the Liverpool Lighthouse is its multi-racial congregation and the black and white diversity of the Love and Joy Choir. It holds before us a vision of what the coming Kingdom looks like. To have such a richly diverse church at the heart of the regeneration of Liverpool with its history rooted in the slave trade shows the transforming power of forgiveness, reconciliation, and justice.

These pages tell the story of a vision made real in and through the lives of Tani and Modupe. It is a remarkable story of love and hope. It is a testimony of leadership. The best definition of leadership is 'followership'. Anyone can call themselves a leader, but if you don't have a following you are not a leader. The watchwords of a leader are 'Follow me'. These are the last words of Jesus in the Gospel of John. Tani and Modupe are demonstrably leaders in the Kingdom of God for they have a following that is dedicated to following Jesus.

Throughout my tenure as bishop of Liverpool I counted it a great privilege to serve in a fellowship of leaders that included Archbishop Patrick Kelly, Akbar Ali and Tani and Modupe.

I counted every visit to the church a great blessing whether to worship or to see yet another initiative in reaching out to the least and the last and the lost.

At my farewell service in Liverpool's Anglican Cathedral I was deeply moved by the presence of the Love and Joy Choir singing *There is a Balm in Gilead*. It's a song about the healing power of the Gospel. In these pages, you will read many examples of how the Gospel brings healing to people. It will inspire you in your own walk of faith and encourage you to go whither the Lord calls you.

There is much to ponder and to learn from here. Other churches that have yet to reflect the diversity of God's Kingdom would do well to study the lessons learnt by Tani and Modupe and their brothers and sisters in Christ.

The Right Reverend James Jones KBE
Bishop of Liverpool 1998-2013

Contents

Transformed to Transform

Introduction

This is a story of love and joy, and of how God built a new church and a new ministry. It began in Nigeria and ended in Liverpool – except the story is not over yet. At the start, there were just two unlikely people - Tani and Modupe...

Tani was born in Ibadan, Nigeria, one of a family of five children. Christianity and music, the two influences that were to play such a key part in his life, were already strongly present in his family. His father, James Olaolu Omideyi, was a trained organist who became a Fellow of The Royal School of Church Music and later Master of Music at St James' Cathedral, Ibadan, Nigeria. His grandfather was an Anglican minister. Tani's family was firmly rooted in Anglican tradition, but at around the age of 15, while at boarding school, he accepted an invitation by his eldest brother to attend a Pentecostal prayer meeting, and had his first encounter with the Holy Spirit.

Tani says: "My life changed in a moment. It became filled with meaning and purpose. I believed that, with the Lord, I could do anything. I began to play 'faith games' with him. There were times when I would say to the Lord, 'Let it rain,' and at other times, 'Let it stop raining,' and it would. I applied my new-found faith enthusiastically to my favourite sport, football. If the team I supported looked like losing, I'd ask the Lord, 'Let them score a goal within the next x minutes,' – giving him whatever time period I felt was appropriate. And sure enough, they scored. The Lord did not have to do it, but he honoured my 'foolish faith'. Even through answers to such seemingly frivolous requests, he was teaching me to trust him with and in everything."

Life certainly became exciting for Tani and his peers. The group of pupils who had come to know the Lord freely evangelised their schoolmates, met to pray and read their Bibles, even sneaking out of school in the evenings to attend revival meetings. Christianity spread like a wave in the school, and some parents began to protest – they did not want their children to be born again, they just wanted them to be 'normal'.

For as long as he could remember, Tani had wanted to be a Chemical Engineer. By the time he was doing his A-Levels, he could see himself attending university in Nigeria, probably Ibadan; doing a PhD and becoming a professor; leading ministry on the campus. Instead, through an unexpected series of events, he found himself on his way to Britain, arriving in 1974 to study at the University of Aston in Birmingham.

Tani, reflecting on that period of development, says: "I learned many important things in those years at university. First, that it was possible to make a covenant with God and, against all challenges, to live up to it. The covenant was that I would not work on Sunday (the Sabbath) but devote it to worshipping him. I learned to keep that vow throughout the four years, neither studying nor getting part-time jobs on Sundays to help pay my fees and living expenses, for which I was totally responsible.

"I also found that God does provide if we trust in him. One incident stands out particularly for me. I was never sure, during the whole four years, where the money I needed would come from. At a particular time in my second year I ran out of money completely. I did not mention it to anyone, but at the next prayer evening at the New Testament Church of God in Lozells, my home church while in Birmingham, one of the mothers greeted me and told me that when they met to pray earlier God had told them to pull together some funds for me. I could not help breaking down in tears of gratitude to God for his care."

Tani adds: "At NTCoG in Lozells and later at the Elim Pentecostal Church in Runcorn, I was exposed to two church congregations and amazing pastors who modelled a different type of shepherding, one based on God's love, which created a fear-free, family environment. Pastor Thompson pastored NTCoG; Pastor Gerald Coates led the Elim church I attended while on an industrial placement at ICI. From the latter I learned what it meant to lead as a servant, which I hope has shaped the way I have subsequently led others in our ministry team."

Another 'God-incidence' took place in 1977. Although Tani was based in Birmingham, he had to do two six-month industrial placements. The first he spent in Grimsby, the second with ICI in Runcorn. On his first Wednesday evening in Runcorn he set out to look for a church. Somehow he was drawn to a small, crumbly building in the Old Town. Inside was a congregation having a farewell service for their pastor, whose wife played the piano. At the end of the service, the mainly elderly folk surrounded him in welcome and began to chat.

Now Tani, growing up in a musical family, had learned the rudiments of piano playing as a boy. As soon as the folk discovered he loved God and could play a little they began to rejoice and praise the Lord for sending someone to help them in their hour of need. Tani suddenly found himself playing in worship and fulfilling a semi-leadership role to a group of Christians he had only just met. It was definitely a wonderful trap that God had set to stretch him. It was also in Runcorn that Tani met the woman who would later become his wife.

****

I was also born in Nigeria in a family of five children. My abiding memory of Nigeria is our house in Lagos, with its pink-gravelled, U-shaped driveway linking the two front gates, dark green casuarina trees and bright red hibiscus flowers – we used to pull these off their stalks to suck the nectar they secreted in their bases. The house was located in what was then a quiet suburb called Ikoyi. During the weekends we rode our bikes up and down the main road – Queen's Drive – and at nights we could look out of our bedroom window and watch the sand dredgers ploughing up and down the lagoon that stretched into the distance on the other side of the main road.

My childhood differed from Tani's in many respects. My parents were Sierra Leonean – my father an economist who worked for a time for the Nigerian government, my mother a teacher. The family relocated to Ethiopia when my father began to work for the United Nations in Addis Ababa; and by the time I completed my A Levels I had lived in Nigeria, Ethiopia, Sierra Leone and Kenya. The family was nominally Anglican but not church going; we were brought up to believe in God but that was that. I know that there were definitely a couple of times in my childhood when I felt a strong desire to get to know God, but I had never been given the gospel; I had no understanding of who Jesus Christ was, and there was no one around who could enlighten me.

Nevertheless, looking back, I could see how the Lord guided me in key ways even before I came to know him. While I was completing my A Levels at school in Nairobi, I resisted the urging of my maths teacher to apply to do maths at Cambridge, and opted instead to study engineering in Edinburgh. I was offered a place in the mechanical engineering department at Heriot-Watt University, but changed my mind and swopped to chemical engineering. Again, as I was coming to the end of my first degree, I turned down a prestigious job offer from Esso in Southampton and opted instead to work for ICI in Runcorn, which is where I met Tani.

At the time we met I was not a Christian, but Tani led me to the Lord and we worshipped together at the Elim Pentecostal Church in Runcorn. The congregation was small and, mentored by Tani, I quickly got involved in serving and undertaking responsibility, as well as developing in other basic spiritual disciplines – prayer, fasting, reading the Bible, sharing my faith with others. A strong spiritual foundation was being laid down that stood me in good stead in later years.

When I became a Christian I realised how God had brought different people across my path to pray for me, show me love and help me along the way to finding him. My ex-housemistress from boarding school had retired to Scotland when I started university there, and we kept in touch while I was in Edinburgh. It was when I wrote to tell her I had accepted Christ that I found out that she had prayed for me for years.

Coming to Christ was amazing – I wondered how I had managed without him for so many years. I was keen to grow in Christ and in the things of the Spirit, and embraced every opportunity fervently. I particularly remember that in the early days I struggled with praying publicly. As was typical in Pentecostal churches, everyone prayed aloud simultaneously and then anyone who felt led to do so stood up and prayed aloud on behalf of the whole congregation. Try as I might, I just could not stand up and pray, and I knew I was losing out because of it. Finally, I set aside time to fast and pray about it. Next prayer meeting, as soon as a suitable pause occurred, I shot to my feet and prayed aloud. That breakthrough gave me a taste for tackling spiritual matters with fasting and prayer.

Like Tani I had had piano lessons in my childhood, and I stepped up and played the piano in worship whenever he was away. I used to visit the church in the evenings to practise, walking the streets even after dark with complete confidence that God would take care of me.

One of the funniest things that happened when I got saved was that I started sleeping a lot, night and day. I had been quite a tense person previously, and now I relaxed so much that I used to drop off right under people's noses, sometimes in the middle of a conversation. Fortunately this only happened when we were visiting or had friends around – I managed to keep awake at work!

****

Tani and I married early in 1979. By this time he was working for Laporte Industries Ltd as a safety engineer; I was still with ICI and had joined a team designing a plant to produce plasticisers, destined for construction in Germany. It was a busy year – getting used to married life; seeking to grow spiritually; longing to see more people come into the church and give their lives to Christ. What we did not know then was that our own lives were about to change in a radical way...

Chapter 1

A New Direction

The first step – out of our comfort zone

It started the year we got married – 1979. That was the coldest January we had had for many years, and on our wedding day six inches of snow and ice covered the ground. I wore two jumpers underneath my dress, hidden by the high collar and flowing sleeves.

The only two people sitting in the church when I arrived were my mother and my brother, who had come from the US to give me away. As time went on more guests arrived, otherwise we would have had a wedding service attended only by the bride and groom, the officiating minister, the best man and a couple of witnesses! After the reception we got a lift to the station, got on the train along with all our presents and suitcases, arrived back in Runcorn and took a taxi to the small flat we had rented. We took Sunday morning off to rest, went to church on Sunday afternoon and were back in work on Monday. In September that year we had our 'honeymoon' – two weeks in Perugia, Italy, staying with Tani's sister, his brother-in-law and their cute baby son.

It was not long after we returned that the Lord spoke to us about Liverpool. We had been supporting the new pastor, Phil Weaver, and his wife Helen in building up the small congregation in Runcorn. Phil, who went on to become Regional Superintendent of the London Region of the Elim Pentecostal Churches, before establishing New Springs UK and New Springs City Church in Loughborough, was fresh out of Bible college at the time. Although he was keen for us to stay and continue the work, we had begun to feel over a period of a few months that God had something he wanted us to do.

One Sunday – it was the 24th of September – Tani came to find me. He had been quite prayerful and reflective since we came back from Italy.

"Let's just spend some time praying," he said. I joined him where he was kneeling at the foot of the bed, and we began to pray, asking God to speak to us and telling him we would obey him. Soon we were led to read the book of Haggai and especially the Lord's promises in Chapter 2. What really jumped out at us as we read were the tenth and twentieth verses that referred to the 24th day of the ninth month. God then spoke about his calling to us. As we talked about it afterward, we knew that God was marking that day apart for us. We could sense that he was calling us to work in a different town or city, and over the next few days it became clear that we were to start going into Liverpool every week and evangelising on the streets.

Neither of us knew Liverpool – Tani had never been there and I had been only once, on a trip to the theatre. It was never our intention to plant a church. We were both young chemical engineers with first class honours degrees, and we naturally expected to progress in that field. But God never showed us the plan, he just gave us one instruction at a time, and we obeyed.

Our enquiries elicited the information that we could buy West African foodstuff on a street called Granby Street in an area of

Liverpool called Toxteth. That seemed a good enough place to start, so one Saturday, armed with a map and a vague shopping list, we drove into Liverpool, found our way to Granby Street, and under the pretext of finding out from passers-by the best shops in which to purchase one item or the other, we started to talk to people and strike up acquaintances.

This was just under two years before the 1981 Toxteth riots, but the evidence of decay, decline and depopulation could be seen clearly in the boarded-up houses, large stretches of waste ground covered with rubble and fly-tipped rubbish, broken pavements strewn with litter – there was litter everywhere - and dog excrement. We were not yet acquainted with Liverpool's particular political and socio-economic problems, but we could see that the Granby area was effectively a black ghetto – virtually everyone, whether resident, trader or customer, was black.

We soon found out that everyone who wanted to buy African food came to Granby Street. You could get yams, plantains – both ripe and green, palm oil, fiery scotch bonnet peppers, okra, various types of edible leaves, highly nutritious *egusi* (similar in appearance to melon seeds), yam flour, *gari* (made from grated cassava that had been fermented and dried), potato flour, creamed coconut, mangoes, pineapples, a whole variety of other tropical fruit, and lots more.

Many of those we spoke to turned out to be mature students from various African countries – Nigeria, Tanzania, Zambia, Liberia; some were merchant seamen spending a year in college, many of them isolated and lonely in a foreign city. Very soon a house group came together, hosted by one member or the other. Virtually all of them lived in Toxteth, a few in student hostels but most others in small, one-bedroomed flats let by private landlords. Any number of us would crowd into the living-cum-dining room, perching on stools and table edges, or sitting on the floor, once all the available chairs were used up. We sang from hymn books and typed out sheets of choruses, and also composed our own songs, read and discussed the Bible, and prayed. Refreshments and chatting followed, before we headed home. We enjoyed ourselves so much we never minded being squashed together. I remember a lot of laughter – not facetiousness, but a real enjoyment in being together in the presence of God.

On the surface of it I suppose Tani and I were not very likely-looking candidates to start a church. Tani had always looked much younger than his age – even when he got into his thirties and had three children strangers still assumed he was a young college student. (I remember him coming home and telling me of such encounters on the bus. He found them rather exasperating – I would be in stitches.) But he had a gift of wisdom and carried himself with the quiet assurance of his faith. I was quiet, introverted and not very confident, something I hid behind a tough-looking (and frequently tactless!) exterior. I had studied in a male-dominated field and felt more at ease dealing with men than women. How was I suddenly to become a leader of women who were around my own age or in some cases older?

Not only that, during our childhood my father had never interacted emotionally with any of us, even though we were loved unconditionally by our mother. The lack of paternal affirmation affected all of us siblings in various ways; in my case it produced a lingering sense of low self-worth. I felt totally unqualified, totally inadequate and often, totally out of my depth. Looking back, it is humbling and reassuring to know that if we are willing to have a go, God can use us in spite of our infirmities, and transform us in the process.

In those early days the men heavily outnumbered the women and one could usually tell the gender of the tenant by the state of the bathroom! Later on we were joined by one or two who lived not far off on one of the streets where the still beautiful former Georgian mansions had been subdivided into flats and rented out. Here the rooms were spacious, retaining the high ceilings and sash windows. Those buildings would have been worth millions each in London. It was not unusual to find a section of a street had been cordoned off while the BBC or some other broadcasting company filmed external scenes of a period drama.

Within some months the group had grown too large to meet comfortably in any flat. Tani wrote around various Pentecostal churches asking if they could spare a room for us to meet in. No reply was forthcoming, so we decided to hire a room on the top floor of the Rialto Community Centre.

The following Saturday, as Tani and I were walking down Princes Road, we encountered a black-gowned priest coming in the opposite direction, and greeted him respectfully. He turned out to be Father Colin Oxenforth, priest of the high Anglican Church of St Margaret of Antioch, outside whose building we just happened to be standing. He stopped to chat and asked us what we were doing; we explained that we were walking around telling people about Jesus, and had been looking for a place to meet. He offered us the use of their chapel (fittingly called Jesus Chapel) at the sum of £2 a week to cover heating and lighting. So the answer to our need had come through an unexpected source, and we had had to meet only once at the Rialto Centre. We were delighted. I wonder if Fr Colin had any idea what would come out his act of kindness. We are so thankful to God for what he did.

Jesus Chapel became our home for Sunday worship for the next two years. It was a really convenient, self-contained building, sandwiched between the large main church and the vicarage. It had its own separate entrance accessed from the gate by a neat path that led past well-kept lawns edged by beds of shrubs. It was just the right size, seating thirty, with rows of chairs on either side of the central aisle, beautiful stained glass windows and an old but serviceable harmonium that we used to accompany our singing. Four radiators provided welcome warmth in winter. We held our Sunday services there and midweek meetings in different homes.

Those first two years of the church plant were really delightful. Unburdened by the responsibilities of a building of our own, we could focus on worship, fellowship and evangelism and we had a lot of fun. We visited and entertained each other (frequently around food), met to compose songs or practise one or other of Tani's musical compositions, which we then sang at special Easter or Christmas events. Members invited their friends along, and the church continued to grow, even though we suffered the seasonal ebb and flow in numbers common in churches composed mainly of students.

Early in this period two key changes happened in our personal lives. The first is that our eldest daughter Tolu (short for Toluwanise) was born. Tani – unusually for an African man! – was a very 'handy' dad, cooking, changing nappies and plying feeding bottles. He had spent a lot of time childminding his eldest nephew, and I learned from him all my early lessons in the basic psychology of dealing with children. The day we brought our first child home was also my first (for me) really hard lesson about sacrifice.

After we had settled for a couple of hours, Tani picked up the car keys and said he was going out.

"Where?" I asked, surprised.

"I told Sister A's children some time ago that I'd take them out on a trip, and I'm going to do it now." Sister A (I can't remember her actual name now) was a lone mother with five or six children ranging in age from seven years upwards, who had joined the fellowship within the last few months.

"But we've only just brought a new baby home," I protested, aghast. I looked down at the tiny, helpless creature in my arms – how on earth was I to manage without support?

"I agreed it with them weeks ago and the children have rung up and accused me of lying to them. I have to go," Tani replied. I reflected with deep indignation that Sister A would have been better employed teaching her children good manners and consideration for others than condoning their unreasonable behaviour. Tani, however, felt honour bound to go, and he went, returning a few hours later. That was but one of the early tests of priority that I had to face.

The second key change was that we both went back to university to do research. Tani started a PhD in the Chemical Engineering department at Salford University, while I branched off into Corrosion and Protection at UMIST (University of Manchester Institute of Science and Technology). After some months of commuting between Runcorn and Manchester, we took out a mortgage on a three-bedroomed terraced house in Old Trafford and moved.

Over the next three years we attended university during the week, travelling down to Liverpool mid-week and at weekends to pastor the group. We hosted them periodically in our home, whether for feasting or fasting and prayer. For years afterwards, both in that house and in our subsequent one, we had a cupboard set aside for all the items of clothing people left behind by mistake, and for some obscure reason never reclaimed!

****

"I promised the Lord," Tani informed me, "that when we got to twenty-four we would get a building of our own."

"Oh," I replied, rather blankly. We had only been living in our house in Manchester for some months and were partway through our first year of university research. What with that and a child about a year old, I was not particularly keen on another change. True, we were averaging twenty four in attendance at services and somehow the church's development seemed to have reached a plateau. We had used up our savings to pay the deposit for the house, and were living on student bursaries. Where would we get the money to buy a building?

While, as was customary with us, I worried about the practicalities of it all, Tani went in search of suitable premises. One day as he was driving around he spotted a little Welsh chapel building on Durning Road in Liverpool's Edge Hill area, and felt the Lord saying that that was the building for us. We found out that it was owned by the city council and had been converted into a school domestic science centre which they now planned to demolish. After some negotiation we bought it from the council for the princely sum of £2,500 (we offered £2000, they asked for £3,000, and both sides agreed to split the difference). Although the sum would be small to us nowadays, it seemed an enormous amount then. Since we didn't have it, the church that Tani's older brother had planted many years earlier in London lent us the money.

We bought the building and the really hard work of refurbishing started. Not a single one of the congregation had skills or experience in construction or related trades. We read up manuals, took advice from electricians, plumbers and tradesmen, and used whatever skills we could transfer from our engineering backgrounds, to do the work. What the group lacked in know-how it made up for in enthusiasm; nevertheless it took two long, quite hard years to finish the work.

We completed the building in early 1984, around the time of the birth of our second daughter. Tani had been keen that we would celebrate Christmas in the building, so, since no furniture had yet been acquired and the gas supply was still to be connected, the women brought pans of *jollof* rice and chicken cooked in advance at home; the men transported tables and chairs from various houses, and we ate sitting around a few portable Calor gas heaters. We were all tired, and just glad that the bulk of the work was over.

This building would be home for our congregation for the next seven years. We called ourselves Christ Apostolic Church, Liverpool (or CAC Liverpool for short), adopting the name of the congregation that had been set up by Tani's oldest brother in London many years previously. Exciting changes occurred in that period. With twenty-four hour access to premises of our own, we could do all sorts of things we had not had the space or time to do before. We started to do evangelism in the area. In those early days we did it door to door. We also distributed leaflets inviting people to all sorts of events. We got some positive responses, and our numbers slowly grew.

Transformed to Transform

Chapter 2

Mixing the 'Colours'

Transforming the composition of the church

Up till this time, the composition of the church had been entirely black, mainly African seamen and students. But this was about to change.

Tani picks up the story: "One day I had a dream in which I saw the church represented as a plate. I saw a hand pick it up and break it into pieces. Then a voice said, 'I will break the body as it now stands, and will bring [indigenous English] into the congregation'. I knew it was the Lord."

Anyone who has ever walked into a typical African church service, especially a Pentecostal one, being previously unfamiliar with the style, will know what a shock it can be to the system. Shortly before coming to Christ I had gone with Tani to his church in Lozells, a predominantly Caribbean congregation, and had been taken aback. Nigerians – and our congregation at this time was predominantly Nigerian – were at least twice as loud, and noise was not the only defining feature!

Tani continues: "We set about making changes to the ways we did church, changing the length and style of worship among other things. The result was unexpected as some existing members became angry and a significant number left. Almost immediately God began to send in indigenous English folk as they got saved and joined the church. God had engineered the space for them to come in and belong. That is why when asked how we have become a fully multiracial congregation I always say it is truly the Lord's doing."

It was during this period, from about 1985 onwards that many, mainly young people who later became the core of the ministry, began to come into the church – Paul, whom the others nicknamed Kracker (because of his cracking personality!); Stephanie, with her sister Rachael and her mother Pearl; Helen and her mother Joan; Mike; Liz, who later became his wife; Jean, who was quickly nicknamed Alfie; and many others.

Paul, one of the earliest English members to join, recollects his early experience of the church: "I came to the church at the age of 17. At that time I worked for a friend, Steve, in his carpet cleaning business, and he was the one who invited me to the church. How he had got acquainted with it I cannot recall. I had not really gone to church as a child, save for the occasional wedding. I had always dreamed of going to a gospel church, but I had an American type image in my mind, or at least what I imagined an American one would be like.

"When I walked into what was then called CAC Liverpool I had a shock. For a start, Steve and I were the only two white faces in the room. All the men sat in the right half of the hall, and the women in the other half. There was a lot of noise going on – beautiful singing, but strange to me because although the hymns were sung in English, a lot of the choruses were sung in Yoruba. After the singing came the word.

"Altogether the service must have been three hours long – no one seemed in a hurry to finish. I found it very African and not what I expected of a religious service! What got through to me, though, was the love and the acceptance extended by the people there. I have a vivid memory of a particular brother, Tony, making me feel extremely welcome. It was this love and welcome that brought me back the following week. In that second week the word began to sink in, and when an altar call was given in my third week, I went forward for salvation.

"It was a full transformation for me, a real change of lifestyle and life concept. I accepted Christ in October; by December I had been baptised by immersion. Some of my old friends thought I was an idiot, but this is what I really wanted and decided to go for it. At that time the pastor's family still lived in Manchester and came down at weekends and for Bible Study on Wednesdays. On Fridays I'd leave work, put a couple of things in a bag and spend the weekend at church, with the family. Friday evening was choir practice (which also went on for several hours). At first I just listened, but after a few weeks Pastor Tani suggested I join. Initially I demurred, saying that I didn't really sing, but he said: 'Join anyway', so I did. This turned out to be the most significant thing that happened in my life after salvation, because it enabled me to find what I believe is my gift."

Joan is another one who experienced a big change in many ways. She says: "I first came to the church in 1986. My own family church was United Reformed – I had attended it all my life, as had my mother before me, and my grandmother before her, and that is where I had taken my children since they were little. That year, my daughter, then seventeen, suddenly started to go to this new one across the road from our house. She had met some of the young people and decided she wanted to go with them. Her character changed beyond recognition – whatever it was just seemed to consume her life. She began to read her Bible all the time. She would bring the young people over and they would invade the front room, sit cross-legged on the floor playing the guitar, reading their Bibles, praying together. They were doing it all the time. I wasn't sure that she hadn't joined a cult, so I decided to go and investigate.

"Well, it was a culture shock. My home church had an elderly congregation; services lasted one hour to the dot. You knew what was coming next because it was the same from week to week. When I got to this other place they were playing the drums, sounding bugles and dancing around shouting 'Hallelujah!' It was so different from what I had been brought up to that I thought: 'This surely can't be church.'

"I rejected it completely. For a long time my daughter Helen and I had to agree to disagree about it. In fact there was a polite but determined stand-off between me and everything that had to do with it. When the young people came around I sat in the back room with the television turned up so that I couldn't hear what they were doing. Unbeknown to me at that time, they were busy praying me into the kingdom.

"After a while I decided to go and check the church out again. This time the pastor preached on the peace that passes all understanding – that you could have this peace of God even though everything around you was chaotic. That really spoke to me because our life was in turmoil at the time. We were a one-parent family struggling to make ends meet, my son had been in trouble with the authorities and had decided that he wasn't going to school any more – all sorts of things were happening. Back at home, as I sat alone pondering what had gone on in the service I felt the Holy Spirit saying to me in an audible voice (very scary) that going to church didn't make me a Christian, and that having a knowledge of God was not the same as knowing God.

"That struck home. I had been a Sunday School teacher, taught children about God, knew about God. Up till then if someone had told me that I was not a Christian I would have been highly insulted. But now I knew that I did not have a living relationship with him, and that my daughter and her friends had something I did not have.

"For eighteen months I kept one foot in my old church and one foot in the new. But the resulting inner turmoil forced me to a decision, and after a discussion with my minister, I committed myself to the new church and walked into what God had prepared for me there."

Many mono-cultural churches, I believe, underestimate the changes required to accommodate worshippers of different cultural backgrounds because they do not realise the extent to which their own expression of worship is influenced by culture or how alien that culture can seem to others. Mercifully the Lord opened our eyes to the need for the changes and we were willing to make them.

I think that being married to a non-Nigerian helped Tani in this regard. Not only was I not Nigerian, I was barely culturally Sierra Leonean either, having spent so many of my formative years outside West Africa. By the time the church started I had lived as long in Britain as in any other single country in my life. I had started picking up Yoruba (his language) after we became engaged, and could understand quite a bit of it, though I didn't speak it particularly well.

This was not through lack of zeal or application on my part. My approach to studying languages was quite methodical – learn the grammar, study the vocabulary. Yoruba, however, is quite tricky – a word spelt one way can have one of several totally unconnected meanings, depending on how it is accented or intoned. The only study books I could find omitted the accenting marks, effectively assuming that the student already knew what he/she was trying to learn.

As a result I had sometimes got fed up of being surrounded by people who constantly conversed in what was essentially a foreign language, and the way this accentuated the feeling of being an outsider.

"What would you do," I remember challenging Tani in the early days of the church, "if people who all spoke different languages came into the church? You would all have to speak in English then, wouldn't you? Why not now?"

Years later, that was exactly what was happening. The beauty of it is that as the congregation became more and more mixed the nature of the worship changed to reflect the different nationalities in the church – African, British, Caribbean – without losing any of its liveliness! We all learned simple songs from the different nations and used them in celebration; our musical styles widened to include rock and reggae along with American gospel, African rhythms and Jewish cadences, as well as traditional British hymn and chorus beats. We were even joined for a period by a group of postgraduate research fellows from mainland China, studying at Liverpool University, who sang for us in their native tongue.

It was not only in worship that this cultural interchange happened; it extended to food, and even the naming of children. As Paul and Helen's generation married and had children, they chose to adopt the Yoruba naming ceremony for them, where the properties of the ceremonial elements of salt, sugar, honey and water were linked with the scriptures to pronounce particular blessings on the child.

Another fact that fascinated the indigenous English church members was that Africans considered names to be very significant, and that the names all had specific meanings that were often related to the circumstances around the conception or birth of the child, or the state of the parents at the time. Paul was so taken with this that he gave his two eldest children Yoruba second names – Oluwafemi (God loves me) and Oluwatoyin (God is worthy to be praised). The exchange flowed the other way as many of the African parents later began to adopt additional English monikers for their children to make life simpler for them at school.

Tani reflects: "The Lord had said in his word that his house would be a house of prayer for all nations, and it became our goal to see as many nations as possible reflected in the congregation. Over the years this vision has remained central to our ministry. We jealously guard that mixed composition in prayer and every other way we can. We believe the body of Christ should have no colour barriers. We have learned how to sacrifice non-essentials for the sake of the gospel. The gospel is the only thing that does not change; the style, culture and everything else around it is what we define and can be changed."

Over the years we have seen how lack of understanding in this area can be a barrier for churches who genuinely long to develop a mixed congregation. In 1 Corinthians 9 the apostle Paul talked about becoming all things to all men so that by all possible means he might save some, while remaining under Christ's law. Some churches, unable (or unwilling) to distinguish between the scriptural and the cultural, tend to see any modification in the way they do things as a dilution of righteousness (these tend to be 'black' congregations) or as odd and foreign (more likely among 'white' congregations).

Bias, we found, also works both ways. Prejudice from the mono-cultural (and mono-colour) indigenous churches towards the believing Caribbean immigrants in the 1940s and 1950s, and later towards Africans coming to the UK from the late 1950s onwards, led to the formation of separate 'black' churches in the UK; in later years prejudice in believing black immigrants towards the indigenous Christians (because of perceived racism and lack of spirituality or desire for God) reinforced it. We encountered many people who had travelled thousands of miles to the UK and other countries only to embed themselves in congregations from their own nation or area of the world.

We knew that this segregation, which seemed normal to some, was directly opposed to God's word expressed in Galatians 3v28: *"There is neither Jew nor Greek, slave nor free, male nor female, for you are all one in Christ Jesus."*

Chapter 3

A Ministry of Praise

Transforming the way we did 'church'

Tani had never been into pop music while growing up, and after making a commitment to Christ he had pulled away altogether from most genres except classical. While at NTCoG, however, he was introduced to gospel music, especially to the music of gospel artist Andrae Crouch, and fell in love with it. Even from the early years of the church Tani had written songs and composed short musicals for special occasions. One Saturday afternoon, he had just left the church on his way to the shops, listening to one of Andrae Crouch's albums for the millionth time.

"Suddenly," Tani says, "I felt God impressing on me that we should set up our own gospel choir and I would conduct and train it. I had no experience of doing this, but I got so excited that I changed course and drove round visiting as many of the church members as I could to tell them the great news."

Within two weeks, we had our own choir. The church was really short of skilled instrumentalists, so we left leaflets in music stores and Christian bookshops inviting any interested musicians to an open day at the church to try out for a gospel band. Stephanie worked as a peripatetic music teacher, so she joined

Tani in assessing those who responded. One of them was a bearded young man with long dark hair and scruffy jeans, case in hand, guitar slung across his back. I had stepped out of the kitchen for a moment and happened to see him come in.

"That one looks a bit wild," I thought. Before long, sweet sounds I had never heard before began to emanate from the worship hall. I popped round to take a look, and sure enough, it was the 'wild' man, Peter, on his guitar. Peter was twenty one, could play piano, keyboard, bass and rock guitar and drums, and sing tenor. He was a key addition to the choir and many years later became our music minister. The other significant addition from that day was Joey Sang, a young man of Chinese heritage who played the saxophone. It was not long before he joined us and became a fully active member of the church, band and choir.

The number of singers also expanded and the choir began to be invited to minister in churches and at events. We quickly came to realise what an effective outreach tool it could be. Interest in gospel music was already growing, even before the 1992 film *Sister Act* boosted its exposure and popularity, so wherever we went we encountered individuals who wanted to join the choir, even when they did not have any relationship with Christ. If they had skills to offer and we felt they were open to the gospel we let them in, and let the love and friendship we surrounded them with do the preaching. Quite a few went on to make a Christian commitment.

After the choir had been going for a while, we decided it needed a new name. It had been called, almost by default, the CAC Gospel Choir, but we wanted something a bit more descriptive and specific. We also wanted it to be Biblical, and to indicate that the choir had some calibre. At practice one Saturday afternoon the members sat around and put forward their suggestions.

"*Qodesh*," said Stephanie, the choir mistress. "It means 'holiness' in Hebrew."

"How about Leviticus?" someone else piped up. The discussion continued as we passed Biblical names back and forth. One brother even suggested, jokingly, that if we called ourselves Gethsemane we would be taken very seriously indeed. After a while Tani spoke up.

"I think I've got a really good name for us." He looked around at the circle of expectant faces. "Love and Joy – that's really what we are about." There was an instant's silence, followed by a chorus of disapprobation. To us the name lacked gravitas. We knew that love and joy were fruit of the Spirit, but compared to the more heavy duty designations we had in mind, it sounded light-hearted, even downright frivolous.

Finally Tani suggested that we put all the names in a bowl. He was not even going to include his own suggestion, but the rest of us (graciously, we thought) said he should. We all prayed, and he then invited Stephanie to pick out one. She opened the slip and read out, almost in disbelief: "Love and Joy Gospel Choir". We all fell about laughing. That became the choir's name; later on, we could not imagine being called anything else.

The time in Durning Road was a great time for us. We learned how to love each other as God's family irrespective of nationality, status or ability. We tried hard to live the early church model in Acts 2, having things in common, enjoying daily fellowship and great accountability to each other. We spent days on end writing and recording new songs for choir and for worship. We learned how to wait on God in days of prayer as needed. We also learned new ways of reaching out to the lost. One of them, which we referred to as 'street singing', was later to be labelled 'Praise Evangelism' by Reverend Dave Cave, a long term friend of the ministry. BBC *Songs of Praise* broadcast it in 2004 when they came visiting us on one of several recordings we have made for the BBC on air and screen.

On selected Sunday mornings each year we would pack our instruments on to a minibus or van and drive slowly through the neighbourhoods with the doors open. The church folks walked behind the vehicles, singing and dancing while the musicians playing, sitting in the vehicles, or sometimes walking behind them. It was never long before we gathered a stream of curious, excited children in our wake. Their parents came out to watch and listen, some still in their pyjamas, readily accepting the tracts, leaflets and invitations we distributed. Our *Praise Evangelism* was particularly successful in an area of Merseyside known as Bootle where we saw many families come to faith through it. Many of them are still with us today, some in leadership positions in the ministry.

****

In 1987 we moved as a family from Manchester to Liverpool. By this time our long-suffering offspring had spent most weekends of their young lives in Liverpool, as well as travelling down from Manchester for the midweek meeting, often getting back quite late at night. The box of groceries, bags of clothes and yellow 'travelling' potty had become standard residents of the car boot. We were becoming concerned about the impact this regime was having on their sleep, and felt it was unfair to continue to subject them to it.

We found a modern semi on a quiet road just outside the Liverpool city border. It had three bedrooms and a back garden that was wider than the others on that road as it was situated on a bend. We were thrilled. It was just the situation we wanted for the children – a pleasant area, a school in the nearby village, church only twenty five minutes' drive away, a garden to play in, a chance to flourish. We met the owner, settled with the estate agent, agreed the moving date (first Monday in July) and sold our house. Then the unexpected happened. On the afternoon of the Friday before the move, the agent rang to warn us that the owner was planning to take the house off the market, and on the Monday morning he confirmed it.

After the initial shock, we had to do some quick replanning, as can be imagined! We couldn't stay where we were because the new owners were waiting to move in. Giving thanks that it was the school holidays, we booked most of our belongings into storage and moved into the domestic area of the church building in Liverpool, taking the minimum needed goods with us. Tani went back to the estate agents, and returned with another leaflet and a viewing later that week in the same area, but this time on the main road.

This second house was also a three-bedroomed semi, but there the resemblance ended. The building was older and far more spacious, with a generous hall and landing. The living room ran straight from the bow window at the front to the patio doors at the back, a length of thirty feet; beyond that the combined patio and garden ran for another seventy. The house could have swallowed the one we had been after with plenty of room to spare, and the back area was about three times as large.

Not only that, Tani had seen it advertised before but at a price outside our range. The same week we were let down, this owner dropped the price by several thousand pounds, bringing it within our range – in fact to the same amount we would have paid for our first choice. Curiously, I was not at all excited or interested. I had dreamed about our first choice house, and looked forward to moving into it for so long, that I was still grieving its loss. On the other hand, Rachael, whom we brought along to give an additional opinion, took one look and simply said, "Buy it. Just buy it." It took some days before it clicked in my mind that indeed it was a great house. We had time to repaint and furnish it without pressure, and in the end our move was delayed by a mere month. There was a lesson there, that God could, at a seemingly most inconvenient moment, take something good from us in order to replace it with something far better.

****

As the church started to reach out into the different communities, we became aware of some of the spiritual challenges associated with preaching the gospel in a society where the knowledge of God and awareness of kingdom values could no longer be taken for granted. Many of the families we encountered were decent and hardworking, wanting to do the best for their children. A number had some sort of religious upbringing, so there was common ground from which the gospel could be presented.

Increasingly, however, we were beginning to meet up with others whose lifestyles were, to us at the time, a complete phenomenon – a woman having children to multiple fathers, none of whom she was or had ever been married to; another, heavily pregnant to one man, leaving him to move in with another. The challenge became how to present the news that Jesus Christ died for our sin, to people who seemed to have no concept of sin.

It was not that they did not have problems – they did. One young woman was distraught because she was convinced that the man she was (currently) living with was cheating on her with someone else. Another confessed to being frequently depressed because by the time she had stocked up with enough cigarettes to feed her forty-a-day habit, and purchased some essentials for the house, she barely had enough benefit money left to buy milk for the children's cereal, so how was she to find money to replace young Johnny's tattered school shoes? To be honest, I felt at times we were dealing with people from another planet.

Soon we began to fill all the seats in our small building, holding well-attended gospel concerts once every month. It was time to start asking God what was next. Our experience with Durning Road had proved to us that we could achieve anything if we committed ourselves as one body to any task. After all, we had purchased our first derelict building and refurbished it ourselves. It was never pretty, but to us it was a masterpiece. As Tani put it, it proved we could achieve anything with God.

Well, God answers prayer, and after five years in Durning Road, he began to move us into the next phase of his plan. By 1989 we had simply run out of space in the building. We ate our lunches outside, and Tani was reduced to holding pastoral counselling sessions in his car. A plague of flies succeeded a plague of rats, and finally we got the message – it was time for us to move.

We had talked about it for a while, but for some in the congregation it had not seemed as if it could really happen. We were still a small church in a run-down building that we could barely afford to maintain to a creditable standard – where would we get the money for an even bigger one? Nevertheless the need had become acute, so (in faith) we started to fast and pray in earnest.

We rose daily at 6am for prayer, and periodically met in each other's homes before going to work. People got together with others living in their area, and each area took it in turn to pray. This went on for months. We had a list of prayer points, and at the top of this was £100,000 for a new building. Looking back, that amount is small in comparison with some of the sums of money we have had to raise since, but at that time it was a fortune. We prayed in faith, not knowing how such an amount was to be raised.

When there is a pressing need there is always a temptation to go for the first available solution. Opportunity presented itself in the shape of a warehouse on an industrial estate in Everton. £64,000 was a high asking price for an empty shell but we were desperate. We agreed terms and the owner promised to have it emptied within a fortnight. The fortnight passed and the premises were still occupied. On the morning Tani was going to meet with him, I opened my Bible without intention to Ezekiel 7v12 and read *"Let not the buyer rejoice nor the seller grieve…"* I knew then that the deal was off – it was not God's plan.

Halfway through the morning Tani rang and confirmed it. The owner had raised his asking price to £70,000, and Tani, having read something along the same lines, had called it off. We were both relieved because the whole deal had felt increasingly strained. Looking back, we would have been totally isolated from the surrounding community if we had moved there, but at that time we were still far from grasping the idea of community transformation in its real sense – we were just looking for a place to have church. God had kept us from making a terrible mistake, but we were still new church building-less. We continued to pray.

Finally the Lord said to us: "Be specific – what kind of building do you want?" One evening the leadership team gathered round the table and on a blank sheet of paper began to list what we considered essential – a sanctuary for worship, obviously; a hall for activities, two rooms for Sunday school, a kitchen, office space for the Pastor, a library, a prayer room, and so on.

Not long after that Tani spotted a notice in the newspaper – a former Presbyterian Church building was being put up for auction. He went along to view it and came back to tell us: "I have found the building." We were too late to participate in the auction but he determined that if it was the building for us it would fail in the auction. It did, and we put in an offer directly to the owner which was accepted. When the rest of us went in we saw immediately that in spite of its derelict state it had all the rooms we had asked the Lord for, either already constructed, or with a space that could be converted to it. The building was on Oakfield Road in Anfield.

We purchased it early in 1990 at a cost of £45,000. Of course the church didn't have £45,000, so Tani and I remortgaged our house to raise the deposit, and the church paid us back over several years. The work of refurbishing it began in earnest in May that year. We didn't know it yet, but this was going to be a significant step in God's transforming work in our thinking, in our lives and in the ministry he had called us to.

Transformed to Transform

Chapter 4

Moving to Anfield

Transforming our location

If Liverpool had a general reputation for being tough, Anfield could have been said to typify the worst in urban decay. Not for nothing had that area occupied a place in the top ten, sometimes in the top five, most deprived wards in the country. Anfield/Breckfield was what came to be known, in government parlance, as a Super Output area – one with multiple indices of deprivation. Even though we did not know the statistics we could see the evidence all around us: derelict buildings, teenagers hanging around the streets at midnight, with their siblings, sometimes no older than three or four years old, sitting on the steps beside them.

Some of the older boys ran errands for local drug dealers, while their parents were to be found in the nearest pub. In fact, the steps of the church building eventually became the territory of the young people in the area – many times we had to pick our way through their midst in order to get into the building to pray!

Even seventeen years later, in 2007, the Office of National Statistics identified the area as the single most deprived in England. City council data[1] confirmed that by 2011, 43% of children lived in poverty compared to the national average of 21%. Across Anfield and its adjacent wards, Everton and Kensington and Fairfield, the percentage of workless adults ranged from 29-39% (against 12% nationally). Violent crime was 36% higher, antisocial behaviour orders 50% more common. Educational attainment was lower than the national average and young people were at high risk of involvement with drugs, gangs and gun and knife crime.

Not only was Anfield the picture of urban decay, it was also known (though we were not initially aware of it) as a stronghold of the National Front. It was only when we began to let other people know where the church was moving to that they began to express horror. Young black students from Tani's school refused all his invitations to attend events there – they did not go into Anfield.

There was an invisible line along Kensington Road that separated the north of the city from the south, and young black Liverpudlians, especially those from Toxteth, generally did not cross that line, for fear of being chased, stoned, stabbed or shot at (with an air rifle, at the very least). We soon came to realise that although the congregation must have been 60% white at the time we moved into Anfield, we were perceived, and referred to, as a 'black' church, and treated accordingly by some sections of the community!

The church building stood at the corner of the main road and a side street of terraced houses. On the opposite side of the main road was a large, derelict-looking building that had been a cinema but now belonged to a uPVC business. Next to the former cinema was a large block with a couple of businesses on the ground floor, and what may originally have been residences on the upper floors. Now there was no glass in the windows, and fires had clearly been started on the upper floors, for we could see burnt beams and smoke stains on the brickwork around the windows. Pigeons flew in and out, making it their home. The whole area had an air of neglect and poverty.

Although we saw all this, we were initially emotionally insulated from it, largely because in those days we simply saw Anfield as the place where our new church building happened to be. It took us years to realise that the Lord had not simply provided us a church building in Anfield, he had actually called us to Anfield.

The church building itself was derelict, and had been so for many years. It had originally been a large Presbyterian church, later it became a builder's yard. Rumour (still unconfirmed) even had it that at one time it had belonged to a coffin maker, though we ourselves were never able to bring a coffin into the building because of the two right angled turns it would have encountered immediately upon getting through the front door. There was no glass in any of the windows, holes gaped in the floor, and the gallery had no floor at all: exposed joists jutted straight into the air.

The existing floorboards were covered with mounds of pigeon's excrement. The banister to the steps leading downstairs was broken. In the basement, whatever flooring had not already been removed was rotten, and the entire floor was covered with rubble. The electricity supply was off, fortunately, as local children had got into the building and broken the mains water pipe, flooding parts of the basement. No matter what, it was the building the Lord had given us, and we knew he had led us to it.

The refurbishment took a year, half the time we had required for the building on Durning Road, although this one was larger. We now counted a joiner and two electricians in the congregation, but we also had a core of faithful, mainly young people who were committed to the work.

When the general work of clearing out the rooms had been completed, Tani divided us into teams, each taking responsibility for a particular aspect of the refurbishment – joinery, electrics, concreting, plumbing, central heating. The only skilled job we didn't tackle ourselves was the plastering. We did get someone in to do the damp-proofing and treat the dry rot, but we suspect that he took advantage of our ignorance and did a partial job.

Most of us were in our normal workplaces during the day. Once finished we would migrate to the church building and get on with our assigned duties. I and Jan, the young Christian sister who eventually married Kracker, were the central heating team. I am pleased to say that the system we put in worked for the whole time we worshipped in that building!

Sometimes the women would cook in huge pots and bring the food to the church. Eating and working together created a real sense of family among us. Only a small number was involved, but we all felt we belonged to the task and that we belonged to each other and felt a responsibility to be present.

Initially the group spent some evenings and all of Saturday on the premises; as the year progressed it became every weekday evening and all Saturdays from morning till midnight. We would pick up the children from school, feed them and drop them off at whichever house they were being minded. Two of the sisters took up the responsibility for looking after the children; as the work became more intense another one kindly minded our own children at home for us, since we lived a half hour drive from Anfield. We would all arrive at the building at, say, 5.30pm, get some food from the fish and chip shop, and work till 3am. Then we drove home, slept for three hours, got up and got ready for the new day.

It is amazing how God provided the strength and stamina we all needed. We were younger then, of course, but it wasn't just that. I believe that it is as Matthew 11v12 put it: *"And from the days of John the Baptist until the present time, the kingdom of heaven has endured violent assault, and violent men seize it by force [as a precious prize—a share in the heavenly kingdom is sought with most ardent zeal and intense exertion]."* (Amplified Classic). It took fierce commitment to do the work, and there was a joy that kept us going, a gift from God in response to that commitment on the part of his people. I believe this extended to those who *'stayed with the supplies'* (1 Samuel 30v24) – childminding, cooking and running errands so the others could get on with the work on the building.

It is important to say, though, that it was not always as straightforward as that. Tani, the true pioneer, was always up for a challenge; I was more inclined to peace and quiet. As a consequence there were several times, especially when facing big works, when I had to submit my unruly will to the Lord's. A dream I had many years ago, during the years in Durning Road, is indicative.

In it we were at an Easter retreat. During one of the services an announcement was made that anyone who wanted to suffer as the Lord Jesus did could go and sign up at the noticeboard. At the end of the session Tani promptly went to put his name down. I admired his zeal but felt no call to emulate it. "Each to their own," I thought.

Later, out of interest, I went to have a look at the list. To my consternation my name was on it. As the time drew near for the suffering to start, my horror increased – how could I bear it? It seemed impossible. And then, gradually, I began to think: "No, I can actually go through with this. It must be possible."

Down through the years, Tani has made a careful note of all the specific promises God has made to him, and gone to them again and again to encourage himself in the Lord, as David did. There is a scripture the Lord gave me that he emphasised to me several times, and that has resonated with me through the years. It is

Transformed to Transform

2 Corinthians 12v9: *"My grace is sufficient for you, for my power is made perfect in weakness."*

Chapter 5

Building by Faith – Trusting God!

Transforming our faith

Soon we became consumed with the work of refurbishment. For many of the younger members of the church, especially those who had joined as young teenagers, it was a real adventure of faith. The church didn't have the finances needed to buy the materials needed for the building, so we compiled a list of everything we needed, split it between different church members, and challenged everyone to pray, look up companies in the *Yellow Pages*, phone and ask them to donate. As the materials came in we would use them to do the things we had to do. Everyone was encouraged to trust God, and everyone rejoiced as we saw the results.

Helen recalls: "I had paint on my list. I had been phoning round company after company without having much luck. I decided on this particular day that I would try just one more paint shop. The manager, who took the call, said that they couldn't possibly give us any paint. I was determined to get something off my list, so I bargained with him, saying, 'Surely you can give me something, even if it is one tin!', which is silly because of course one tin wouldn't do very much at all. Eventually he relented and said, 'Okay, you can have two tins; come and collect them.'

"Liz picked me up in her small run-around car and took me down to collect these two tins. What I hadn't realised was that the company shipped paint, so he'd actually agreed to give me two large drums. When we got there he said, 'Where's your vehicle?' and I replied, 'No, it's alright, we'll carry them into the car.' It soon became clear that there had been a misunderstanding! Then he agreed that they would deliver the paint. We had to decide what colour we wanted so we asked for a magnolia and a beige because we thought that would go far.

"After he had delivered the paint, Pastor Tani asked if it was possible to change one of the colours, and the man just delivered the third drum in the colour that we wanted, without charging us a penny for any of the paint. That paint actually painted most of the interior of the building. That was really funny and went far beyond what we expected or thought that we had asked for. The generosity is something I remember, that so many people, companies and businesses – not necessarily large ones – gave when we asked of them."

It was not just paint we were given – as we prayed and trusted God, companies donated free concrete, furniture, glass, and much more. A store that was redecorating its premises offered us the carpet they were replacing. It turned out to be just the right size and in excellent condition (the carpet remained in place for twenty six years). A group of four organised a bike ride from Bradford to Liverpool. On the back of this we all went out and asked for all types of sponsorship.

Greenberg Glass generously donated a ten foot diameter round pane of glass for the window aperture high above the altar. Helen and Stephanie had the task of applying a stained glass effect to it, and spent weeks carefully working on it. One evening as they put the finishing touches we heard a cry of horror. Helen, forgetting that the pane was lying on a metal grill rather than flat on the table, had leaned on it, and it had shattered. Cap in hand, we went back to Greenberg Glass, who kindly replaced the pane.

It is difficult to overstate the growth in faith and confidence that we enjoyed as we saw God's hand moving to provide in answer to prayer. We did what lay within our power, and God stepped in and did the rest.

****

There were two aspects to the welcome we received in the area. Although we rarely laid eyes on the perpetrators, we often came out of the building to find a car window smashed, a tyre punctured, a vehicle smeared with broken eggs or the remains of someone's chip-shop meal. Racist abuse was shouted out of passing cars. I think it is fortunate that so many of us could not understand the Scouse accent well enough to know what was being said!

There was the added vexation of constantly receiving parking tickets on match days, as the building was bounded by double yellow lines. We never knew what we would find when we emerged, and we simply did not have enough manpower to keep a constant lookout while we worked. We just learned to give God praise, call the AA and get on with things. Eventually we got to know the traffic wardens and after pleading with them and explaining what we were doing we came to an arrangement where they left the identified vehicles of church members alone. I suppose over the years the neighbourhood got used to our presence and the incidents abated. They did not cease though – I remember one year after bonfire night we found a pool of fuel and a burnt match on the top step outside the main door. Someone had been intent on arson – fortunately whoever it was had used diesel, not petrol, so the attempt had failed.

On the other hand we could never forget the welcome we received from the Christian community. Several church ministers came to formally welcome us into the area. The owner of a corner shop a few blocks away brought a large pan of soup one Saturday to sustain us as we worked.

Not all the challenges we faced during the period were from outside. It is interesting that at this period we experienced a significant drop-off in the engagement of the congregation (a sifting time for the church). For seven years we had worshipped in the refurbished Welsh Church building in Durning Road, and it was the lack of space that had forced us to look for alternative premises. As we got down to the hard work of building, we found that less than a quarter of the congregation committed themselves to the labour. Many fit and healthy young men and women showed up for services on Sundays but never responded to any call to contribute to the work.

This had an interesting and inevitable result. The people who shared in the fellowship of labour and shared the frustrations, joys and laughter of it all, really bonded and developed close relationships with each other, while those who did not get involved felt increasingly isolated. Many of them eventually drifted away. It is not surprising that when we finally moved we were so few that we needed only the first few rows of seats to hold the entire congregation, and even then we could barely hear each other singing!

It was also in this period that we got acquainted with another phenomenon – the most difficult members of the working group to get to commit to turning up on time and doing their allotted share were those who were unemployed, and unlike the rest of us had no other daily work commitments. The excuses were unfailing – they had to sign on, this was their day for visiting their mother, they were tired because they stayed up late last night watching TV or visiting friends, and so on and so forth.

Initially it was baffling; later on we began to understand some of the deeper reasons behind it.

Andy Beckett, in an article in *The Guardian*[2] in 2015, described the impact of the government's monetarist policies in the 1980s on places like Liverpool. He refers to discussions between Patrick Minford, a monetarist academic lecturing at Liverpool University during the early 80s, and Alan Walters, who had become Chief Economic Adviser to the Prime Minister, Margaret Thatcher, in 1981. Minford, providing consultancy on macroeconomics to Walters, came up with what was dubbed the Liverpool Model.

According to Beckett: In a strikingly short 1981 pamphlet titled *The Problem of Unemployment*, Minford wrote: "Estimates based on the Liverpool Model suggest that a combination of a 15% cut in real social security benefits ... and a reduction in the union [wage] mark-up to its level in the mid-1960s...would reduce unemployment in the UK by around 1.5m by the mid-80s."

He points out that although, during the 19th century, Liverpool had been one of the richest ports in the British Empire, by the 1980s that prosperity and prestige were long gone. Britain's maritime trade had moved steadily to other ports on the east coast, closer to Europe. Moreover, the factory jobs that were meant to replace the dock work had been disappearing too, with Liverpool plants "increasingly regarded as disposable branch facilities by manufacturing conglomerates based elsewhere." Liverpool's population had been dropping faster than in any other city in the country: from a peak of almost 900,000 in the 1950s to under 500,000 in 1981.

Beckett continues: Later in our conversation, though, Minford conceded that the sheer scale of the shake-out in Britain's jobs market had surprised him. The initial versions of the Liverpool Model had assumed, as did many Thatcherites, that the country's "natural" rate of unemployment was low, and therefore purging the economy of inefficiencies with monetarism would mean, at worst, hundreds of thousands of redundancies – rather than millions.

"In the Liverpool Model, we were too optimistic about the speed with which the economy would…come right," Minford admitted, "although we were closer than many of the pessimists." Then he paused, untypically: "The bit we were way out on was unemployment."

In fact, the impact of monetarist policies on unemployment levels in an already struggling city like Liverpool, was disastrous. Unable to find work, many of its residents were forced onto benefits. The benefit system could rightly be described as a trap because of the way it was structured. Any individual who attempted to top up his or her social security income by taking on any kind of work was allowed some paltry sum, £10 or £15, which was probably eaten up by travel to and from the workplace, before losing in benefit, pound for pound, whatever was earned through casual employment. The only legal alternative was to be fortunate enough to land a job which paid the rent and all the household bills, fed and clothed the family and covered childcare if young children were involved. There were no stepping stones between the two extremes.

It was not surprising that there was a hopelessness, a growing feeling of worthlessness, in the attitude of the unemployed that manifested itself as a lack of motivation for any gainful occupation. This was particularly so for the long-term unemployed who were probably watching the pattern repeating itself with their children.

"You have no idea," one young man confided, "what it is like not to be able to find a job for a long time. It saps you, saps your energy. You don't want to get out of bed, because there is nothing to get up for. It is then that things that create any kind of routine, that give you anything to look forward to, become obsessively important, like your favourite TV show, signing on and getting your dole cheque, meeting up with your friends for a pint."

This was someone from an affluent background who through simple bad luck had been unable to find a job during a stint between one period of education and another. Our locals in Anfield, burdened with shame and diminished self-esteem, were probably beyond articulating such feelings.

It dawned on us that even if jobs suddenly became available for all, many of the unemployed would be unemployable because they had lost their work ethic. There were households in Liverpool, and in Anfield in particular, where there were two grown up generations that had never held a job, and a third generation growing up with no employed role model in the home. As I write this, we are hearing reports of households containing four workless generations.

****

We formally opened the building on May 19, 1991, on the sixth birthday of our third daughter, Igbaladun. As we gathered for our first Sunday service, God's Spirit moved among us, as if to say "Well done!" for having completed this task he had set us.

Transformed to Transform

Chapter 6

Bethel Community Projects
A wider ministry taking shape

"**R**ight," said Helen, "we're up to day five. That's five cups of lemonade, four Brussels sprouts, three chocolate biscuits, two scoops of ice cream and one banana." She pushed these items across the table to Lisa, the girl she was addressing.

"I hate Brussels sprouts," moaned Lisa, a slim, fresh-faced girl of fourteen.

Everyone else crowded round, laughing. It was a church games evening; Helen's house group was setting the challenge that month, and it was the turn of the youth group to respond. This particular game had been thought up by Helen and was based on *The Twelve Days of Christmas*. Every time they went through the song, Lisa, the youth group's nominee, was given more items to eat or drink – if she failed the challenge the points would go to Helen's house group.

These evenings, like so many of our fellowship activities, took place in the church basement. The room was quite large, about 12 metres by 14 metres, connected to the kitchen beyond it by a door and a serving hatch. The six concrete pillars that supported the ceiling had been thickly padded with foam and faux leather so that children (and adults for that matter) could run around safely.

In the two years since we started worshipping in Anfield, God had steadily added people to the body. The seats had gradually filled to the back, and people had started to sit regularly in the gallery. (These were not necessarily latecomers; they were another phenomenon – the 'back of the church' Christians. This cohort liked to come to church but preferred to spectate rather than participate; it was as if they did not want their lives changed by the Holy Spirit.)

We had started Junior Church and house groups; we held Bible Study classes and prayer meetings. We even took on a paid youth worker, Katie, who ran a youth club and summer play schemes for the youngsters in the neighbourhood. At one time house groups took it in turns to cook the Sunday meal, so that as many of us as could crowd in ate downstairs after worship before going home. The gospel choir had grown and was travelling from place to place in response to invitations.

Less than a year after we moved to Anfield, two women in the community had approached us. They had been looking after a group of about eight particularly troublesome teenagers, trying to keep them occupied and off the streets. It was a mixed group of young boys and girls aged between thirteen and fifteen, some of whom either had given up going to school, or were persistent truants. They wanted to hand these teenagers over to us to look after and our two youth leaders, Paul and Keith, accepted the challenge. Lisa, the hater of Brussels sprouts, was one of this group.

Paul and Keith set up a youth club in the basement and set about building relationships with the group, taking them out, playing football and table tennis with them, forming a youth choir. Initially they saw the church building merely as a warm place to hang out and let their hair down, but then they came to realise what we were and what we were trying to do. The group underwent a transformation and within a year had become the church youth group.

At their first Christmas time with us the church threw a party for the senior citizens in the community. We can still remember the apprehension and astonishment in the faces of the old ladies as the very youngsters who had harassed them for years handed them tea and cake, singing: "Jesus, Jesus loves you; yes he does."

It was a rich time of ministry to the youth. Tani and I, who by now had gone into teaching, particularly encouraged them to go back to school. Most of the boys were not keen, but several of the girls did go back. In the fullness of time a number of these girls went to college, gained qualifications and found stable jobs. One in particular responded so well to the challenge that she completed her GCSEs, did A Levels, went to university and gained a degree in paediatric nursing. She later completed her Masters and is now the first Advanced Nurse Practitioner in General Surgery within her field in the country, holding a high-level nursing post at a world-renowned hospital in the city. She said later that her commitment to her education became such that the most severe punishment her mother could threaten was to keep her off school!

It would have been nice to say that all of these young ones continued to walk with Christ into adulthood, but for the boys especially, idleness, peer pressure, poor influences in the home and the habits of a lifetime proved too strong. Once one or two backslid the rest followed suit. A descent into crime landed one of them in prison, but even from inside he wrote to what was left of the group to say how much he regretted wasting the opportunity he had had.

In the course of their work with the youth, Paul and Keith kept coming across young people who had been thrown out of their homes and had nowhere to go. Paul eventually suggested that the church start an advice centre. He researched the provision available to young people at the time and concluded that this was a gap. Having left his job with the city council, he started work as a full time volunteer adviser providing accommodation advice and signposting to young people. We called it Bethel Housing Concern – it was a table, chair and telephone in a room in the former church building on Durning Road, which we had not yet sold.

Paul very quickly realised that these potentially homeless young people had very limited rehousing options.

"There's just nothing available for them," he told Tani. "If we want to really help we will have to provide the accommodation ourselves."

After some discussion they agreed that he should approach the Liverpool Social Services' Leaving Care Team, as they were responsible for arranging accommodation of young people at risk of homelessness. Paul arranged a meeting with the Team Leader, Steve.

Paul recalls: "To be honest, when I first started explaining the idea, he was unencouraging to the point of resistance. We got halfway through the meeting before he finally realised that he was not dealing with a young entrepreneur who was possibly looking to cash in on the needs of the young people. After that he was more willing to listen."

What really clinched the matter was his attending a service we held to celebrate the homeless and highlight their needs. By the end, he truly understood that we were simply a church trying to do some good in the community. His attitude changed and he went away to see what he could do. Not long after, Social Services offered us some young people to accommodate. We leased a house in Wavertree from Derrick, a businessman in the church, took on some members of staff, and our accommodation project, Bethel House, was born.

Gradually this first house filled up. Initially we used a model of partial support on the basis that the residents were old enough to regulate themselves. Some of the referrals, however, needed round the clock supervision and more intensive one-to-one work, so we rented a second house to provide this. In time the first house was phased out. We used the name Bethel Community Projects to cover not only Bethel House but also the other activities we continued to run, mainly for children, back in Anfield.

Around this time a 14-year-old boy, Mark (not his real name), was referred to us. Mark was the baptism of fire for the accommodation project. He had been evicted from countless care homes. An innocent looking, dark haired youngster with light green eyes, he trusted no-one and felt the need to test any love or interest in him to destruction to prove that it could not be genuine. He had a gas-sniffing habit; under its influence he became so volatile that even his mother wanted no contact with him.

Because he was so disruptive, it was decided to move him onto different premises, away from the other residents. The domestic quarters in the Durning Road building were converted into a flat for him, and Paul was assigned as his full-time support worker. Social Services offered us approximately £1000 per week to look after him, as they only expected him to stay for a week. After six months they asked to revisit the terms of the contract because it was costing them too much!

Our methods in those days were simple – we provided them with relationship, with a church family, a unit they could become part of. They were invited to people's homes for meals, brought along to our fun days, encouraged to join the youth choir. None of us had studied behaviour management, nor were we experts in Safeguarding, but we were able to impact the lives of several of these boys in a way that became a lot more difficult in later years.

Sadly, the anxiety around the safety and rights of children and young people, and the subsequent proliferation of red tape within the statutory sector have led to a formal, arm's length approach to caring for them that actually robs them of the very thing they need most – warm, caring, stable relationships with adults who have their best interests at heart. Paul saw himself as being a big brother to these youngsters, we saw them as young people whose lives could be transformed by God's love, and that made what we offered different. He and our other workers were prepared to go that extra mile, and even though Mark, like others, was eventually moved on, their time with us made a real difference in their lives, and this gained us a good reputation in the eyes of the Leaving Care Team.

It is possible that if the funding for Mark had not been stopped, and if he had not been moved into a flat of his own too soon, his life could have been completely transformed. Unfortunately statutory sector decisions are often made on the basis of finance, rather than the real needs of vulnerable clients, and can be short-sighted in the extreme. After Mark left us he drifted into crime and was eventually arrested for burglary and sent to prison. In the longer term, it would have been cheaper to have left him with us.

Nevertheless God had the last word. Nearly twenty years later Mark turned up just as we were finishing the Sunday morning celebration. He wanted to let us know that he was doing well, had a job, girlfriend and child, and had never forgotten the love he had been shown while with us. It is really encouraging to realise that the ministry's input into his life had not been in vain.

Chapter 7

A City Divided

The need for transformation

From physical appearances alone, Liverpool would have been judged as being very religious – it seemed to have church buildings around almost every corner. The city had seen revival in the time of Evan Roberts and the Welsh Revival of 1904-05, and we were many years later shown records of the impact[3] that Evan Roberts' preaching had had in Anfield. By the time we moved into Liverpool, and into Anfield, what was more evident was religion and the religious divide between Catholics and Protestants, which was a legacy from the Irish ancestry of a significant proportion of the population.

These divisions were still very strong, especially in the north of the city. Orange Lodge marches were regular annual events. The line that divided the 'Catholic' area of North Liverpool from the 'Protestant' area ran through Everton. We had learned to be sensitive even in the matter of choosing and using colour schemes for notice boards, posters, leaflets and so on, so as to avoid any appearance of sectarian bias. Orange stood for Protestant, green for Catholic, just as red stood for Liverpool Football Club and blue for Everton.

Nonetheless, we were later to learn two significant things. The first was that during Billy Graham's Mission England in 1984, there were more decisions recorded from L4 (the Anfield postcode) than from any other postcode in the country. The second was from a 2014 mapping of, ironically, the atheist hotspots in England and Wales[4], which showed that of all the areas in England, Liverpool recorded the highest percentages of people who believed in God.

Be that as it might, Liverpool was a city of division – division between north and south, division based on football, division based on denominational affiliation.

There was territoriality, even within areas, wards and neighbourhoods. Oakfield Road was the separating line between two adjacent wards, Anfield and Breckfield. We soon found out that people from one side of Oakfield Road did not mix with people from the other side. In fact, as soon as we began to work with the group of young people from the Breckfield side, brought to us by the two concerned women, the young people from our side (the Anfield side) stopped coming.

In Liverpool, you either supported Liverpool Football Club, or Everton, and the indoctrination started young. There were parents who would not dress their children in the colours of the 'other' team. It was, just, acceptable to support a team from outside the city, unless of course it was Manchester United. Tani, a lifelong supporter of the latter, had the constant challenge of defending his allegiance in the face of widespread and unceasing disapproval from the congregation!

The most shocking division we could see in the city, however, was based on skin colour. Apart from within and around the one area, Toxteth, where they seemed to be contained in practically a ghetto, the indigenous black population of Liverpool seemed to be virtually invisible.

A City Divided

Ray Costello, in his book *Black Liverpool: The Early History of Britain's Oldest Black Community 1730 – 1918*[5], points out that there has been a continuous Black British community in Liverpool dating back more than two and a half centuries, with some black Liverpudlians being able to trace their roots in the city as far back as ten generations. And although the Atlantic Slave Trade might have been the cause of black people settling in Britain from the 18th century onwards, by no means all of them were slaves or servants.

As Ray explains, by the late 18th century, Liverpool had the monopoly of five-eighths of the European slave trade. Ships set sail from Liverpool, buying or capturing young Africans from the West African coast and then embarking on the infamous 'middle passage' to the West Indies. Having offloaded whatever survived of their human cargo for auction to plantation owners, they would load up with goods and commodities which could be sold back in Britain. The sea captains would also bring back personal black servants and slaves from the West Indies whom they sold off at some point to the township's wealthy merchants anxious to show their new found status by following the new fashion of owning black servants and slaves.

Ray further explains that during this period, the British saw it as politically advantageous to encourage African chiefs to send their sons to be educated in Britain, in the hope that they would receive an indoctrination favourable to the British viewpoint. These would–be students were usually entrusted to the care of the ships' captains. (Of course, there was always the danger of their being sold as slaves by unscrupulous sea captains who considered one sort of black much the same as another.)

Some of these students eventually returned to their home countries, but others chose to stay, finding wives and homes in the city, adding to the growth of the Liverpool black community.

Subsequent to this there was a succession of African students from well-to-do families wishing to complete their education in a place where they would find relatives. First they were drawn by the bonds of kinship; later they saw it as a safe haven for black students visiting Britain as the social climate for blacks worsened during the progression of the 19th century[6].

During the American War of Independence (1775–1783), a proclamation was issued by the British Royal Governor of Virginia, offering freedom to all slaves who deserted their American rebel masters. This was to deal with the fact that the British forces were being seriously outnumbered by American rebel forces at a time when reinforcements took a long time to arrive by ship from Britain[7].

Following the British surrender, many of these thousands of 'black loyalist' ex-servicemen were forced to seek a new life in British-held territories such as Canada. Those who chose to come to Britain swelled the numbers of black poor in the country, many of them being reduced to begging in the streets when they failed to find employment[8].

One of the largest single contributions to the Liverpool Black population is that of black sailors. Even during the Slave Trade the West African coast was notorious for its reputation as 'the White Man's Grave', and as coastal peoples had a tradition of seamanship, trading and fishing along the considerable stretches of the West African coast, Africans were sometimes recruited as free sailors in their own right, to replace English sailors who had died or deserted[9].

Those who survived would sometimes disembark in ports such as Liverpool, having been laid off and awaiting a return journey home or another voyage. Post Abolition, black seamen were employed on ships travelling between Liverpool and West Africa, partly because of the inhospitable climate of the West

African coast, and partly because, after 1910 at least, the Africans provided a cheap source of labour[10].

As a consequence of all these movements of people, the local black population became very mixed in terms of country of origin, in colour (they married among themselves but also intermarried with members of the local white populace), and in social class. However, the levelling-down effect of the propaganda of the Slave Trade upon all black people settling in Britain in the eighteenth and nineteenth centuries meant that most black people made their homes in the poorer districts of Liverpool[11].

It was not that immigration into, and settlement in, Liverpool was a strange phenomenon. Ray Costello describes Britain as an island peopled by successive waves of immigrants, the majority of whom have gradually been accepted into mainstream British life. The Huguenots, fleeing religious persecution in France, settled in the North-West during the seventeenth and eighteenth centuries. The steady trickle of Irish immigration into Liverpool became a flood during the 1840s and 50s as a result of the Irish Potato Famine in 1845, settling in the poorest parts of Liverpool, including the black settlement area.

Other groups of immigrants included Scots, Italians, Norwegians and Chinese, each, like the black community, having their own settlement areas in various parts of the city. Friendships between poor whites and blacks formed, often in conditions of abject poverty. However, the negative view of black people spread by the plantation owners and others making a living out of the slave trade fomented attitudes of racism that prevailed even among the poorest in society[11].

The struggle for universal suffrage, from the early nineteenth century Chartists onwards, provided poor whites with the machinery to better their lot. With the passing of time and improving conditions of the poor, more poor whites were able to pass into the middle classes[12], a facility denied to blacks as the overriding barrier to acceptance within society became skin colour. The descendants of settlers from other parts of Europe were assimilated as Liverpudlians, while the black community, settlers of even earlier origin, was ostracised[13].

What was so shocking was that even in the 2000s, this situation persisted. We had only seen the 1981 Toxteth riots and acknowledged its root causes from a distance, being still resident in Manchester at the time. Now we were face to face with the situation facing Liverpool-born black people. I remember Tani applying to a funder based in London (the project was to work with locally-born ethnic minorities), and one of their officers coming up to meet with him for a chat before their panel considered the application. She arrived early so she could walk round the city centre and get a feel for it. By the time she arrived for the meeting she was furious.

"Where are the black people in Liverpool?" she raged. "One can go round London, Birmingham, Manchester, Leeds city centres, and see them working in businesses, in retail, in banks, in public buildings, playing a full part in the life of the city. Here they are hidden!"

We were obviously not responsible for the situation, but we didn't get the funding.

We had become used to hearing about, and observing racist attitudes in North Liverpool, but it seemed that the whole of Liverpool had a problem with racism that was rooted deep in its psyche, and would take the power of God to transform.

Modupe and Tani

**Love and Joy Gospel Choir
in action at Greenbelt**

The refurbished exterior of Liverpool Lighthouse

An event at Liverpool Lighthouse

Love and Joy Ministries' 30th Anniversary Celebration, 2010

The Oakfield Road building,
now owned by a local business

The Temple of Praise Leadership and Management Team

Harmonize Academy recognised by Ofsted as an 'Outstanding School'

A panorama of Bright Park

Actress Jennifer Ellison, staff and pupils of Harmonize Academy

First spiritual home: Jesus Chapel at St Margaret of Antioch

Waterfront Gospel Festival, 2007, in front of Liverpool Maritime Museum

The church's first real home in Durning Road, now converted to apartments

Chapter 8

A Church Divided?
Towards Unity
Transformation in the way churches relate

As mentioned in the previous chapter, one of the divisions we observed in Liverpool, especially when we moved into Anfield, was the division along religious lines – Protestant and Catholic. Research[14] suggests that the massive scale of Irish immigration in the mid-1800s fuelled sectarianism which eventually escalated into such violence that areas of the city became 'Catholic' or 'Protestant'. It is said that by the 1850s 'the working-class was split in Liverpool in a way that was unique in England.'[15]

The origin of sectarian division can be said to have been economic and xenophobic, as well as religious, owing to 'one workman frequently regarded another as a jealous competitor rather than as a colleague in a common struggle.'[16] After World War II sectarianism began to decline in a piecemeal fashion, but it remained significant well into the 20th century. Even in the 1980s and 1990s, Orange parades took place periodically in the city, and still do today.

In 1975 David Sheppard became the Anglican Bishop of Liverpool, and Derek Worlock the Catholic Archbishop of Liverpool in 1976. The strong relationship that developed between the two has been credited with helping to calm spiritual divisions in the city[17]. Their ecumenical vision and conduct were such that they became affectionately known on Merseyside as 'fish and chips'[18]. According to Reverend John Williams: "The biggest impact on the decline [of sectarianism] was the Great Mersey Miracle. The great friendship, trust, and common bond shared between Sheppard and Worlock cascaded down to the ordinary parish clergy. 'If they can do it so can we', was the attitude..."[19] Furthermore, the two had taken over during an economic recession, and their joint efforts to tackle the social and economic problems that threatened the livelihood of their people gained them much credibility, affection and respect[20]. They made the churches seem relevant to the real problems in people's lives[21].

What about relationships with and between local churches that did not necessarily fall into the mainstream Anglican or Roman Catholic categories? In our experience they still operated very much as separate entities. One indicator was the ease with which disaffected members could go from congregation to congregation, complaining about the one they had just left, with no communication between the ministers to check facts. There was little mixing among churches of different national origins. The same tendency to division that characterised the city seemed also to operate within the body of Christ. But God was at work.

Dave Cave came from Bradford to pastor the Rock Church from 1977 to 1983, and then led Anfield Christian Fellowship from 1983 to 1994. He and John Cavanagh, who became the first chairman of *Together for the Harvest,* the local alliance of Evangelical churches, both confirm that from their perspectives there was a long-standing movement towards unity within the city. John had left his employment with ICI in the mid-1970s and started working full time as evangelist with a Brethren church in Bootle. The Brethren church was quite strong on Merseyside and had done a lot of church planting. John's involvement with Liverpool came through his connection with that church.

John says: "Even then (in the 1970s) there was an appetite in Liverpool for working together across denominations. There was a whole number of initiatives, leading to prayer and/or evangelism or events at the Philharmonic Hall and the Anglican Cathedral. But the big event was Mission England with Billy Graham in 1984, which actually covered the whole of the Northwest and involved about 3000 churches working together to put it on."

John was the Visitation Coordinator for Mission England. Since the idea was that everybody in the Northwest would have a personal invitation, the churches were encouraged to knock on doors. A million homes were visited in three weeks. Mission England ran every night for eight nights at Liverpool Football Club's Anfield stadium, and cost the princely sum of £0.5 million.

He continues: "There was a lot of unifying going on around the project. It seemed to me that one of the big issues then was that people would unite around projects, but once a project was gone the unity dissipated. At the same time there were people in the city who were working and praying for unity over many years."

The unity initiatives included John 17:21, a prayer group. A number of evangelical churches formed *The Way for Wirral*, holding periodic tent missions. *SHINE* – St Helens Inter-church Neighbourhood Evangelisation, was strengthened by *Mission England* – they were, states John, really in advance of everyone else in terms of their unity.

A young man called Steve Whittall, whose pastor father was a key figure in the Elim Church and widely respected among the city's churches, was instrumental in starting up Merseyside Evangelical Alliance Trust. *MEAT*, as it was known, was considered the local expression of the Evangelical Alliance UK. Its remit was representative rather than pro-active, and garnered a membership of sixty churches who were also members of the Evangelical Alliance.

In this period a minister called John Partington (who became National Leader of Assemblies of God UK) came from Bedworth with six families or so to plant a church in Liverpool. A friendly and charismatic personality, he met up with Len Grates from City Church, Dave Cave and David Elms, the pastor of Kingsway Christian Fellowship.

The four started monthly meetings called North West Christian Leaders' meetings, drawing attendees from further afield than Merseyside: Blackpool, Chester and Manchester. Part of the vision for NWCL was the evangelisation of every person in the area, and they laid some of the foundations that were later adopted by *Together for the Harvest*.

What about us in Anfield?

In 1992, Tani received a strong impression from the Lord that the churches in our locality should start to work together. He approached the Methodist Church, led at that time by John Joughin, Richmond Baptist Church, Rev Dave Cave, and Rev Steve Pierce, who was in charge of Christ Church Walton Breck.

The result of the meeting between the four church leaderships was a series of combined open air events in Stanley Park featuring music, singing, dance and mime with face painting for children, handing out information and tracts to those who stopped to listen. It was just a way of saying: "The (combined) church is here for you." We called our local initiative *ASK '92* (Ask, Seek and Knock).

In 1989, a seminal book called *Dawn 2000: 7 Million Churches To Go*, by Dr James Montgomery, came out. It laid out a strategy for discipling nations, planting churches and putting a viable witness to Jesus within reach of every individual. The book highlighted the experiences of a group of church and mission leaders in the Philippines. In 1974, seventy five of these leaders committed themselves to work towards the goal of a church in every neighbourhood by the year 2000. This would mean growing from about five thousand churches to fifty thousand in twenty six years. By 1988, the church was not only on schedule to reach this goal, but actually to exceed it.

This message went global and a team from *DAWN 2000* visited the UK. A meeting was arranged in Birmingham called *Challenge 2000*, and 700 leaders met and set goals to plant 20,000 new churches by the year 2000, resulting in one church per 1000 of the population.

John takes up the story: "I went to the *Challenge 2000* meeting. Some representatives from *SHINE* attended, but I was the only other person from the whole of Merseyside. Coming back, I decided I was going to have to do something about this. At this time I was on sabbatical from leading Brook Fellowship in Runcorn, and praying about what to do with my future. Once as I prayed I looked up. There was a map of England and Wales on the wall, but because Wales wasn't part of what we were doing it had been ripped off. The background of black showed through like a great black arrow pointing, and at the very end of the point was Liverpool. I had asked: 'Where do you want me to be, Lord?', and when I saw this I thought: 'This is what I should do.'"

John spoke to various leaders, and from November 1992 arranged a meeting of leaders, saying "Here is the vision – let's plant churches." He says: "At that time a young man called Nic Harding had just moved into the area and started a church called Frontline Church. At a meeting of 20 to 30 leaders, he said something along the following lines: 'How can we do this, really? We can't plant churches – we need to work at relational unity with one another. This is the key – the key is doing things together.'"

Within the next two years some key decisions had been made. There had been a number of initiatives and groups with overlapping membership and leadership, all aiming to do the same thing. It was agreed that there would be one organisation with a mandate from all the leaders; it would be the local expression of the Evangelical Alliance, it would subsume MEAT and fulfil the role of NWCL. A team of four was appointed to start setting the vision and leading it. This team was John Cavanagh, Tani, Nic, and Ray Smith from Elim. The organisation was named *Together for the Harvest*, or TFH, for short.

Over the next decade and more, TFH really brought the evangelical churches together in Liverpool, building relationships between church leaders, developing a joint vision for the city and its region – that of reaching every man, woman and child in the Mersey region with the gospel. It set about building capacity in churches through training, and spearheading joint initiatives and events, by far the largest of which was Merseyfest[22]. This had a lasting and measurable effect on the way the evangelical churches related, moving Liverpool at the time ahead of many other cities in this respect.

Of course, some of the challenges local unity movements such as TFH will face on an ongoing basis include keeping in tune with what God is doing nationally; remaining sensitive to where their local constituents are at, so that the movement is seen as relevant, and adapting their arrangements so they can effectively engage with the ever-widening range of ministers and churches God is bringing into the city.

It would be impossible to name all the church leaders and churches we came to know and interact with in one way or the other as a result of the move towards relational unity. Nor were they confined to evangelical circles. Ministers grew to know each other, preached in each other's churches. We became friends with Bill Bygroves, the senior minister of Bridge Chapel and chaplain to Liverpool Football Club. We loved his unique, 'pop gun' style of preaching, and he in turn invited Tani to preach and the choir to minister at his church.

Several of the ministers we came to know served as trustees on one or other of our boards, including Ray Smith, Dave and Tina Cave, Kelvin Boulton from Holy Trinity CE Church round the corner on Breck Road, John Manwell (who eventually set up The Well fellowship). We had got on really well with Ray, so much so that at one point we had discussed merging our two local churches, and after he and his family relocated to North Yorkshire a strong relationship continued to subsist between Tani, John and Nic.

One person who gave us and our ministry great support and encouragement over many years was Bishop James Jones, who succeeded David Sheppard, consenting to become our patron. We had just got to know the Dean of the Anglican Cathedral in 2011, Justin Welby, when he left to become, first Bishop of Durham, and then a year later, Archbishop of Canterbury.

Chapter 9

What Next, Lord?

Transforming our outlook

Back to Anfield. By this time the Lord had brought us a long way from where we started – so many changes had taken place since we received that first call in 1979. Our outlook had changed completely from the closed-door, mono-colour concept of church that would have been the norm for many black-led churches at the beginning. Our church was multinational, 60 to 70% white, and our worship reflected the influences of the different nations represented among us, and even of those passing through.

We had learned to do outreach attractively through 'praise evangelism' on the streets. We took the gospel out through the ministry of the choir and its supporting 'acts' – drama, dance and mime – to all sorts of venues, including secular ones. They were received as enthusiastically at festivals and weddings as at revival meetings and praise and worship gatherings – individuals who would never think of darkening the door of a church danced, clapped and rejoiced as much as anyone else.

(Incidentally, we found that the choir got some of the most enthusiastic receptions at Catholic weddings. The congregation would be up and dancing from the moment the band struck up. This openness to all denominations had some interesting repercussions. Tani was once accosted in the street by a longstanding member of a church in the south of the city, and berated for mixing with Catholics. This gentleman seemed to consider Tani to have more or less betrayed the faith.)

Our young persons' accommodation project was meeting the needs of young care leavers, and we had started other smaller projects by this time. One, *Open Hands,* started as a ministry of visiting the sick and elderly in hospitals and at home, bringing them flowers. For a period we also had a small shop selling Christian and other gifts in our old building in Durning Road – we named it *The Greatest Gift*. The aim was to interact with the community in Edge Hill and introduce them in a gentle way to the gospel message. Alfie spearheaded the visiting for *Open Hands* and ran *The Greatest Gift*. It must be said that we did not consciously classify any of this work as social action, we simply responded to need.

Nonetheless, at this point very few of the church members lived in Anfield. Two families had moved into the area when the church moved – the rest came from other parts of Liverpool, from adjacent boroughs (as we did), from the Wirral, even from Manchester and Fleetwood. We travelled in, had our meetings, and left. We were meeting to worship in Anfield, but much of our ministry to observed needs took place elsewhere, and reached people elsewhere. We did not have a particularly local focus. But God was working, and things were changing.

One major change that took place within our first seven years in Anfield is that we registered *Love and Joy Ministries Trust*. Up till then, we had been using the charity number of Tani's brother's church in London, treating it as a sort of umbrella – at least on paper. However, it was becoming clear that we needed to establish a separate legal identity of our own, and in 1995 we took the plunge and established the trust, naming it after our gospel choir.

We now fully entered the demanding world of statutory regulation and charity governance; on the other hand our official charitable status enabled us to apply for grants (admittedly small amounts to begin with) and donations towards our activities for young people. We were later, over a period of twenty years, to replace that trust with a charitable company limited by guarantee, to set up a second charitable company, to acquire another trust passed to us by Liverpool City Council, and to set up an educational trust.

We also changed the name of the church to Temple of Praise, recognising the fact that we were not really representative of any of the Christ Apostolic Churches[23] we knew about, nor was the name 'Christ Apostolic Church' one that had any meaning for the people we were reaching out to.

Gradually we began to look around us and see the disadvantages and needs in Anfield. It is true that we had been based there for some years, but we still thought that God had given us a building in Anfield because he loved us and was meeting our need for a place to have church! It was, from a human point of view, a rather strange choice for a thoroughly mixed congregation – Anfield was a deeply racist community, whereas Edge Hill, where we had been based before, did not have that feel. (Later we realised that God had moved us to Anfield in the same year that Liverpool Football Club bought its first black player, John Barnes. As the years progressed we began to see more and more black people move into the area, including contingents of asylum seekers and refugees, who were often housed in one of two grim high-rise blocks in Everton, the neighbouring ward.)

As we observed the very serious needs right around us, we began to experience a deep questioning – what were we, as a church congregation, really there for? Who were we? We could see the destitution in the community – physical and financial, moral and spiritual, and we felt helpless. One particular event really spoke to us in that period and it arose from the Assembly of God's *JiM* (Jesus in Me) Challenge. We had registered with *JiM* as one of the participating churches.

At the end of the challenge we received a response card from the administrative centre in London, sent in by a man who lived two or three streets away from the church. When he was visited, we found out that he did not know the church existed, although we had been in his neighbourhood for seven years. That shook us. For the first time we began to feel that we were actually irrelevant to the lives of the community around us.

Tani says: "I was going about, visiting and ministering to the flock, but I felt torn in my spirit. I began to ask myself the question: 'Whom am I pastoring?' I felt God say to me: 'Within a mile radius of this building there are 50,000 people. If I bring even 5,000 into your congregation, what of the other 45,000? You may feel you are doing well but to me the other 45,000 matter as much as the 5000.'"

We were not the only ones questioning our purpose. All over the city, God was stirring up the same question in the hearts of church and ministry leaders. Dwight Smith of Saturation Church Planting International, based in the US, and co-author of *Journey into Mission Church*, was a man of God who had gone through some of this journey with church leaders in the States.

Tani says: "Dwight had come to the UK wanting to engage with church leaders on this matter, and found us at that stage where we were of a similar mind. Four of us – myself, John Cavanagh (leader of Brook Chapel, a Brethren church in Runcorn), Ray Smith, who led the Elim Pentecostal Church in Liverpool, and Nic Harding of Frontline Church, went away with Dwight Smith to pray together and spend time really being challenged about the purpose of the church. It was this exploration that helped shape the *Together for the Harvest* agenda."

This exploration was having a tremendous impact on us personally and on the church. We all had that sense of being at a place where we were having very little impact in our city, a city that was in many ways broken and divided. The wider church did really seem irrelevant in the city context, just as we felt we were irrelevant in our community.

At this same period the Transformation videos were doing the round of the churches. These documentaries, presented by George Otis Jr of The Sentinel Group, showed the impact on cities and communities as the Christians united and prayed. As we watched the stories of what God was doing in Cali, Colombia; in Fiji, in a small village in Kenya; in a community in Guatemala, we became excited about what the power of God could do in an area.

Tani continues: "All this helped to lead us into what we were later to understand as the transformational church – a church that saw itself not as a unit that was there to sustain itself but rather as a plant of God in the community, intended to bring about change. The theology was still not totally clear but it was very helpful to gain a better understanding of the Biblical context of the church – it would help us to fully shape what we were to become."

Transformed to Transform

Chapter 10

The Purpose of the Church
Transforming our understanding

Tani states: "A key part of this further transformation in our thinking was coming to understand that the purpose of the church is to fulfil the ministry of Christ.

"We Christians, even leaders, talk about what the church is: the body of Christ, the bride of Christ and so on, but hardly ever address its purpose. I remember going to Kenya on a mission trip just before the presidential election in 2007 that subsequently led to so much bloodshed. The Lord had really challenged me, when I waited on him, to speak on the purpose of the church. This was the first time that I had had to spend time looking at how I would present the purpose of the church to places in Africa where, for instance, a particular form of the gospel, particularly the prosperity gospel, had totally penetrated."

Tani continues: "It is clear that in human terms, the instructions that control a person's body come from his or her head. Christ is the head of the church, his body. The body of Christ should be following the instructions from its head. It follows logically, then, that in order for the church to really understand its purpose, it has to understand the purpose of the head. The Lord Jesus said he would only do what he saw the Father doing – he came to fulfil what the Father commanded. And that is what he had passed onto us. So the church truly exists to fulfil the mandate of Christ.

"So what did Christ come to do? We all know that Christ died for us. We are obviously not going to die again for ourselves – that part is already done. But what is the full mandate of Christ? It is common for salvation to be preached through the context of Christ dying to bring mankind back to God. Yet in Paul's letter to the Colossians 1v19-20 he brings up the concept of Christ dying to reconcile all things back to God. The redemptive power of Christ goes beyond just man – it's the whole of creation that Christ seeks to bring back to God.

"This helps us to understand what our mission is. We might think that our only purpose is to go and preach the gospel to others so that they will be saved. But surely Christ came for more than that. The Lord led me to look at Christ's triple-faceted ministry as prophet, priest and king."

****

"The Bible clearly describes the Lord Jesus as the Prophet, the King and the High Priest in the order of Melchizedek (Acts 3v22, Revelation 17v14, Hebrews 5v6).

"If the church was to fulfil Christ's mandate, it needed to be prophet, priest and king. Unfortunately, we had come to a time in the church where the concept of the God of salvation was so personalised that it had no relevance to other areas of life. Christians no longer saw their roles in any way as leaders of nations, leaders of cities, leaders of regions, leaders of communities. In a sense we had almost gone back to what happened when Israel said to God, *'We don't want you to rule over us any more – give us a king like other people,'* (1 Samuel 8 v 19 - 20). So the prophet that God had raised to rule over them was exchanged for an elected king. But in the Scriptures we see the God of Abraham, Isaac and Jacob as a God who ruled. His intention has never changed – he made mankind to live under his rule.

"We are puzzled, for instance, when our governments keep enacting secular and humanistic laws; we wring our hands and pray, hoping for the best, and yet so often seeing them turn out for the worst. But where is the church in bringing that prophetic voice to the community, to the city, to the government?

"Christ is King, so what about our responsibility to be king over all the areas of community and society? And what about the priestly role, the intercessory role of the church in bringing the community to God, repenting on behalf of the community, and so on? Transformation, therefore, is not just about doing social action, it is about understanding and fulfilling our intercessory role as priest, our kingly role as ruler, and our prophetic role in bringing God's word. The body of Christ needs to understand all these aspects, not remain in the mind-set of just snatching people from their sin and locking them up (inside the church building) while we abdicate our real roles and responsibility as the body of Christ in the world that God has made.

"So that is really at the heart of the transformational agenda – recognising that the church was not a little remnant in one corner but actually the body of Christ carrying out the mission of reconciliation that Christ came to perfect in his body.

"Another key part was also understanding that the church exists in different forms. There is the worldwide body, but in the Bible we find the concept of the city church defined – a church that exists in a geographical area and operates in that context.

"We grasped that, yes, there are different groupings of the body in the city using different names, but for the church to fulfil the purpose of God in a particular area, the congregations have to understand how critical the unity of the body in that area is, because it is no longer about the church leaders doing things, it is about everybody in every church becoming empowered to be effective and to achieve. It is also about those churches coming together collectively to really impact their area. The importance of the city church, or the area church, becomes paramount.

"That is why as Temple of Praise we could not travel along the journey of understanding the purpose of the church without giving the same attention and focus to the city wide church. Our purpose in Anfield was linked to our purpose in Liverpool – one without the other wouldn't make sense. We began to understand that we (Temple of Praise) were only part of a church that God had put into our region, and for us to achieve what God purposed for us we had to work with others so that collectively we could fulfil the purpose for which God had put us here.

"Our understanding of unity was this – other churches weren't competing, they were part of the same package of being church where God had placed us – being church in Anfield and being church in Liverpool. So the work with TFH really strengthened the work we were doing – suddenly we were no longer just a church in Anfield doing its own thing, rather we were part of a city wide church that had brothers and sisters in every part of the city, and together we could really bring the change that God purposed for our city."

Chapter 11

From Purpose to Vision
Transforming our focus

The growing understanding of our purpose in Anfield had a revolutionary effect on our outlook. Now Anfield was not just our location, it was our parish, our responsibility. What could we do about the problems we could see all around us? How could we help the teenagers who sat on our steps, swigging from bottles of cider and cans of beer, smoking, calling to each other in their own particular vernacular, seemingly indifferent to all about them?

How about the boys who rode their bikes up and down the streets with silent purpose, stopping by one car or another with dark-tinted windows, pulled up briefly at a street corner or pavement? A wound-down window, a quick exchange, and the car would zoom off down the road, while the biker took off on yet another drug delivery errand. We had got used to seeing pairs of trainers hanging by their laces from the telephone lines, ostensibly to indicate that drugs were available on that street. We were even told that the brand of trainers indicated the type of drug on sale.

Girls as young as fifteen pushed their little infants around in prams, infants who would in all probability become single teenage parents in turn. How could we open to their understanding even the possibility of a different lifestyle? And what about the parents, drinking away whatever means they had night after night in the local pubs, seemingly indifferent to the needs of the children they had brought into the world? Many of the young people had told us that there was no point going home at night – there was never any food in the house.

We realised that if we were to do anything that would make any difference in the lives and situations of the community around us, we would have to do it on a fairly large scale. The church building which seven years ago had seemed so ample for our needs, we now realised was woefully inadequate – we needed lots more space.

Early one evening, Tani sat in his car outside the church with Mike, the church treasurer, discussing this very fact. As they chatted, they looked across the street and saw something they had not noticed before – that none of us had noticed. There was a 'For Sale' sign on the old cinema building directly opposite. Was this God's provision for our need? Tani came back and shared the matter with the elders. Not only that, he asked the elders to go away and pray individually, and ask God to speak to them specifically about the building and what would go on there. When the eight elders fed back, every single one had received quite specific dreams or pictures about it, some of which were confirmed by members of the congregation who did not even know what was afoot.

At this point Temple of Praise had about £100 in its bank account. Nevertheless, Tani went to meet the owner of the building, Arthur, to negotiate a price. Arthur was closing down his uPVC business and retiring. His daughter worked for the pub just up the road from our building. The pub wanted to expand and was offering Arthur, cash down, a sum £20,000 higher than the one Tani mentioned. But Arthur said to Tani: "Look, I've been watching you people for the last six years and have seen what you are doing. The community needs that more than another pub. I'm offering you the building. I'll take a mortgage out on it myself – you pay me back when you can." And they shook hands on it. Within a short time, God had provided the building.

John Manwell, who later chaired *Together for the Harvest* after John Cavanagh retired from the role, recalls: "I remember when Tani invited a group of us ministers to come and see the building. This was in late 1997 or early 1998. The outside of the building was grimy and dilapidated – it had probably not been cleaned since it closed down as a cinema in 1960. Beyond the shop space at the front were two or three massive workshops full of dust, uPVC shavings and offcuts from double glazed units. From inside it was apparent that the shell of the building had been left to go to rack and ruin.

"The tiered seating area on the upper floor had been stripped back to the wood and was strewn with lumber. The balcony rail was missing, leaving a precarious drop from that level to the ground floor. The previous occupier had built a self-contained two-storey office block in the gap between the tiered seating and the rear rooms of the building, leaving a parking space for the vans that brought supplies to the premises. From this area of the ground floor we could see right up through the building to the heavy vaulted ceiling made of old-fashioned steel-reinforced plaster.

"Tani walked us from one derelict space to another, sharing his vision: 'We'll have a project here to upskill young people,' he said. 'We'll use this space for IT training, and run a project to give homeless people the skills they need to maintain a tenancy. We'll have a café over here, where we can mix with the community. This will be the auditorium. Here we will have the recycled furniture outlet …' and so on. It was immense. The memory of that visit is always with me and is a constant reminder of how dreams and visions can become a reality."

At that time we and our minister friends had no idea just how immense the work would be. For a start, even after purchasing the building, we would have to raise well over a million pounds to complete its refurbishment. And we would have to do so in the teeth of opposition from within the very community we were looking to help.

Once we had decided on the building we printed leaflets and went knocking on doors on various local estates to explain what we were planning to do, and asking for the residents' views. The majority expressed their joy that something would be done at last to address their problems and to provide for the needy and increasingly disruptive youth in the area.

It was a particular set of people who considered themselves guardians of the community, who were supposed to represent the interests of their people, who reacted with open, determined and implacable hostility. They summoned us to a meeting, which Tani attended with two of the elders, and asked who we thought we were, to imagine we could come and do something in their community. They then told us in no uncertain terms that unless we were prepared to set up a company fifty percent owned by them to purchase the building, they would ensure we didn't access a penny of regeneration money to fix it up.

We were stunned when Tani reported back, but once again we were tasked with seeking God's will on the matter. I was so spiritually revolted by the idea that I don't think I even brought myself to pray about it at all. When we next met, Mike recounted a dream he had had. In it, an item had been delivered (it was not clear what it was). Some of the elders were trying to fit it into a space in a room, but it was the wrong size and shape and wouldn't go in, no matter how hard they tried. I had walked off from the start and refused to join them. Mike awoke while they were still debating how to get it to fit.

This intervention, which we knew was from the Lord, confirmed our decision to politely but firmly refuse our opponents' demand. We didn't know how God would make a way, but we trusted he would. We decided to go ahead with the purchase of the building, and continued to pray and plan. Not too many weeks after, both Orange and BT (now O2) contacted us separately about the possibility of putting telecoms masts on the flat roof. We listened to their offers and told each that if they were prepared to give us five years rent up front they could go ahead. They accepted, and that gave us the money we needed to cover the deposit for the mortgage.

****

Refurbishing this building, which we initially called TOP Centre, was a completely different experience from our previous two ventures. For one thing, the scale of the work was different. The first phase – the front section of the building under the flat roof – could be done by the church because it was mainly clearing, cleaning and painting, and was accomplished in a relatively short space of time.

Phases 2 and 3, which comprised the rest of the building, required major construction work, which involved the whole package – architect, surveyor, quantity surveyor, a feasibility study, a tender process to find a suitably qualified and competent construction company, and a principal contractor. All of this required money – a lot of it. Some of it would be raised by the church, but a large amount would have to come from Europe, so a major funding application had to be put together to the

European Regional Development Fund, along with ones for smaller amounts from other sources.

It was not just the size of the task that was different. The whole process was actually redefining what we were as a church. Increasingly our prayer focus turned towards the community, pleading with God to change their lives, transform their outlook, rescue them from sin and the apathy of despair, break the hold of drugs, alcohol and other forms of bondage in their lives. The other focus for prayer was of course the TOP Centre, what was needed to complete it, and what God willed it to become. We were used to fasting and praying, but now the focus was completely outward.

The fact is, the change in the church was even more fundamental than the one we had experienced when we refurbished the church building in Anfield. At that time we were preparing a building for our own activities, now we were consumed with something that was not about the congregation. The leadership, and all the others who felt most closely involved, were able to ride this wave of change, but there is no doubt that less robust souls within the body were affected by a sense of alienation from what was going on, and there was not much we could do about it.

The front section being completed, we started running projects. The recycled furniture outlet started with passers-by dropping in to browse through our small collection of bric-a-brac, hearing our story and bringing their old furniture for us to sell towards our fundraising effort. It became a focal point for engaging with the community and encouraging them to get involved with what else was on offer in the building.

Upstairs, using second hand furniture and even older computers, a range of life-skills courses were launched – a tenancy support programme that not only helped homeless young adults find accommodation but also equipped them with the skills they needed to hold down a tenancy: budgeting, shopping, cooking, cleaning, paying bills; IT courses combined with CV writing support and work experience placements; volunteering. We shared the vision for the centre with everyone who came in, and when they offered their services as volunteers we snapped them up. Even though it would take five years to complete the refurbishment of the building, individual lives were already being impacted and transformed.

Transformed to Transform

Chapter 12

Liverpool Lighthouse: It's Not a Church Building!

Transforming our activity

Tani recalls: "One of the first questions I had to settle with myself when Lighthouse started was this – suppose we did all this work with the community, and not a single one of them ever became a Christian or joined Temple of Praise, would we continue? And the answer had to be 'Yes'."

This was no longer about filling church seats – it was about bringing the kingdom of God to the community. The Lord Jesus's manifesto in Isaiah 61 included binding up the broken-hearted, proclaiming freedom for the captives and release from darkness for the prisoners, replacing the spirit of despair, rebuilding ancient ruins and restoring places long devastated. This was such an apt description of the state of our community. We needed to proclaim the good news, but in a way that impacted people's lives and was relevant to them where they were at. Whether or not they subsequently followed Christ was between him and them.

For a start many people, from previous experience or from indoctrination and prejudice, were suspicious of church anyway.

Others saw church very much as another social provider, like the benefits office or the NHS – there to supply a need without the need for any responding commitment or obligation on their part. That is why we felt it was important to promote Liverpool Lighthouse as our multi-project centre, not as a church.

There was another reason – many secular grant funders were so prejudiced against anything that had to do with faith that even knowing we were a Christian group was enough to scupper our chances. It did not matter that the activities themselves were non-religious, were open to anyone and everyone, and that our aim was to turn round broken lives – there was an immediate assumption that we would use the funds to proselytise. It became very useful to have an organisation that was perceived as being separate from the church to bid for grants and manage the activities in the building – that was Liverpool Lighthouse Ltd, which we constituted as a charitable company in 1998/1999. As Jesus said, we had to be wise as serpents and innocent as doves.

But just because we did not promote Liverpool Lighthouse as a church did not mean that we did not see it as part of the church. We bathed the building and its activities in prayer to the point that even non-believing visitors said that they could feel something different in the building – they loved it but couldn't explain what it was. We could have told them that it was the presence of the Lord!

And we saw this having an impact. In 2003 a two-person team came to interview Tani about the work of Liverpool Lighthouse for their book, *Creating Space For Strangers*[24], written on behalf of *Tearfund*. David Evans was a Baptist minister who had previously worked for *Tearfund* and gained considerable experience of social action; Kathryn Scherer was a Christian writer of both fiction and non-fiction. The book aimed to gather together stories of churches around the world who loved their neighbours, stories that would inspire fresh thinking about mission and the church. One example referred to in their book, is that of Peter (not his real name).

Peter was placed with Liverpool Lighthouse by the probation services fairly early in the refurbishment process. At that time his life was really going nowhere, but he knew he wanted things to change. He started off carrying out general maintenance work and helping with very basic aspects of the refurbishment of the building, including painting. However, Tani had made it a habit to share the vision for the building with everyone who came within reach, and it was not long before Peter himself became enthused with what he was hearing.

Because he felt so much a part of what was going on, he continued to volunteer at Liverpool Lighthouse once his probation was over. Eventually it became possible for Liverpool Lighthouse to offer him a job doing what he had decided he wanted to do – running the maintenance team for the building. Not only that, the organisation sent him to college to get the relevant qualifications, and paid for him to learn how to drive. By this time Peter had begun secretly reading his Bible, and eventually made a commitment to Christ. His encounter with Liverpool Lighthouse led to a change in his life that has lasted to this day.

Peter is only one of the many instances of transformation that we saw taking place. Individuals came in, were welcomed, encouraged and supported, given opportunities, equipped with the skills they needed, but more than that, made to feel loved and included, regardless of the state of their lives. This is what led many to make commitments to Christ, and even those who did not, would come back in later years to tell us that they could never forget what the Christians at Liverpool Lighthouse had done for them.

****

All the while this was going on, we were fighting the battle to complete the refurbishment of the building. We needed money from two sources – the European Regional Development Fund (ERDF), and match from the Single Regeneration Budget (SRB)[25], and we needed to secure the latter before we could go for the former. As any application we put in for SRB money would have to be validated by one or other of the subgroups involving our opponents in the community, it already seemed as if we were facing an insurmountable obstacle.

They even invited us to take up the services of one of their appointed consultants to carry out the required feasibility study for the building, assuring us that we could apply to one of their pots of funding for the £12,000 consultant's fee. Once the study was completed, they informed us that there was no money available in the pot, presented us with the £12,000 invoice and demanded immediate payment. We had to scramble together every penny in the ministries to pay them.

Not all the 'community guardians' were ill-disposed towards us. One local councillor in particular has proved himself the soul of kindness and supportiveness to us down through the years. Those who opposed us, however, seemed unrelenting in their aim to thwart what we were doing. Not only that, they seemed to exert a baleful influence over other groups and individuals who, left to themselves, would have been happy to work with us.

One evening, the church leadership met in the refurbished front section of Liverpool Lighthouse to pray. During the prayer, the Lord gave Tani an impression that everyone present should put all the money they had with them into a bowl, pray over it and put it on the altar table in the church as a memorial offering. It was a real act of faith for one couple, Peter and Helen, who had just drawn out the money to pay their childminder for the week. Everyone complied, however.

Within the following weeks and months, things turned around. An alternative regeneration partnership subgroup emerged and validated our application. The application went off and was successful, as was the ERDF bid. The remaining phases of the refurbishment moved forward. An award-winning local PR company, Finch Partnership, did our branding design free. It was the founder who suggested that the building should be called Liverpool Lighthouse, as its purpose was to be a lighthouse for the community.

When the scaffolding went up around the building for the very last stage – the cleaning of the outside and repair of gutters, it was like a visible sign to the powers, both earthly and heavenly, that God had vindicated his name and his people. Once again his will had prevailed and there was nothing anyone could do to stop him.

Transformed to Transform

104

Chapter 13

A Wider Influence

Transforming perceptions by the statutory authorities

Liverpool Lighthouse opened formally in November 2003. We were blessed to get a member of the Royal Family to open it – HRH Princess Alexandra, the Duchess of Gloucester, who was visiting Liverpool at the time. The opening had been scheduled for July, so when the Lord Lieutenant's office rang to let us know there would be royalty visiting Liverpool in the autumn, and asking if we wanted them to be involved in the opening, we told them, regretfully, that it would be too late.

A few weeks prior to the opening date, a section of the old reinforced plaster ceiling, which had been passed as safe by the architect, detached itself and plunged, bending a piece of scaffolding and embedding its spikes into the wooden floor beneath. All work in the auditorium stopped. The old ceiling had to be brought down, and Tani had to spend time raising a further £40,000 to replace it with a modern suspended structure. The delay meant that the opening was rescheduled for the autumn, so we got back to the Lord Lieutenant and said, yes, we would be delighted to have the Princess!

It was a remarkable event, the climax of so many years of prayer and hard work. Tani had taken the brunt of the responsibility for it, chairing both of the boards, running the ministries, pastoring the church, spearheading the fundraising and also fulfilling the role of principal contractor for the refurbishment, saving the ministries the £70,000 it would have cost otherwise. There were days when I myself wondered how he could cope.

I remember escorting Princess Alexandra through the main doors into the auditorium, and looking down at the tiered seats packed with guests, the walls freshly spray-painted with the art deco features picked out in contrasting colours, the floor thickly carpeted, the new suspended ceiling pristine, the choir robed and ready to sing, flowers massed around the lectern, Tani standing to welcome everyone – it seemed like a dream.

To us, the attendance of the Princess was an added sign of God's favour. Even a number of our opponents honoured their invitations and turned up. One or two had the grace to admit they had been wrong about us, and offered to work with us in future.

Within a year or two of the opening our projects had really taken off. Initially it seemed we could never fill all the space available in that large building, but eventually we had to internally restructure to create more rooms, and convert little nooks and crannies into storage areas, if nothing else. We applied to UfI (University for Industry) to become a *Learndirect* centre, and became the first centre on Merseyside to be granted a licence to run *ELLIS* – an online English course for speakers of other languages.

We developed it ourselves into a blended learning course, combining taught classes with online work; over the years we added integrational activities and many other forms of support for our learners, the large majority of whom were asylum seekers and refugees traumatised by their experiences of escaping from their home countries and forcible separation from their loved ones. Even when UfI decided to consolidate all its *ELLIS* offer and gave the one contract for Liverpool to Hope University, we continued to develop and run our ESOL (English for Speakers of Other Languages) Integrate course with other sources of funding. Today our waiting list stands at almost a hundred and fifty.

We had opened Liverpool Lighthouse as an urban gospel arts and community centre. The emphasis on urban gospel music and arts really influenced the development and operation of the centre for the next thirteen years; we not only used the genre to engage with isolated and disaffected groups of all ages, we also incorporated music and arts elements into virtually every community project we set up, whatever its main objectives, or placed music and arts at their very core. It also allowed us to establish our standing as the UK's first dedicated urban gospel music and arts centre.

For this reason, when we observed the number of truants on our streets, we went to their schools and offered to take these disaffected youngsters on a pilot project based on sessions of hip hop, rap, DJing, singing, song writing and learning instruments. These were interspersed with personal development sessions where they could look at their own behaviour, try to understand the reasons behind the anger simmering just below the surface of so many of their young lives, and learn more constructive ways of expressing or dealing with it. It was exhausting for the workers, but rewarding too, as by the end of each cycle they could see the youngsters gaining in self-confidence, developing skills, saying please and thank you, and addressing others without swearing!

The project had a new intake every six weeks and this quickly exposed a weakness. The young people were being sent back to school just as they were beginning to change – many of them retrogressed and returned to truanting. Longer periods were needed with us to embed changes, and some actually could not flourish in mainstream school at all. We developed a full time programme, incorporating English, Maths and appropriate vocational qualifications, went to the local education authority and asked them to start referring excluded pupils to us. Thus the urban gospel music and arts-based *Harmonize Alternative Education* project was born, taking pupils not only from Liverpool but also other Merseyside authorities and schools. This was our flagship project till it successfully transitioned into an alternative provision free school seven years later.

In 2004 we started an ambitious four-year gospel music project named *City Sings Gospel*. The idea was to build the capacity for gospel singing in schools, businesses, churches and communities across Liverpool, building up to a local, a national and an international festival of gospel music, the last of these to coincide with Liverpool's 2008 *Capital of Culture* celebrations.

The first year was spent recruiting gospel choir trainers and training them. In the second year the trainers went out and began setting up gospel choirs in schools and churches. The local festival took place in Liverpool Lighthouse. The third year, 2007, coincided with the 800th birthday of Liverpool as a city, and the 200th anniversary of the passing of the Abolition of Slave Trade Act. We named it the *Amazing Grace Festival*; the programme running over seven months. As part of it Liverpool Lighthouse hosted the annual *National Gospel Summit*, compered by Juliet Fletcher[26]. This gave us recognition in the UK gospel music scene, as hitherto its focus had always been in London, and when outside London, in Birmingham or Manchester.

Now Tani had had a vision of a Christian civic service of repentance for the city's part in the transatlantic slave trade, and to celebrate the lives of the millions of slaves who lost their lives at sea. This was to take place in 2007, so as to precede the

Capital of Culture celebrations. It was fitting, he believed, for this service to take place at sea, and this meant approaching the Royal Navy to host it.

In faith, he contacted the Ministry of Defence, and having secured a meeting, he jumped on the train to London to present his request. He was then referred to the Naval Regional Headquarters for Northern England, based in Liverpool, commonly known as HMS Eaglet, for a meeting with the then Naval Regional Commander for the North of England and Isle of Man, Commodore John Madgwick. Again Tani presented his vision and request. At the end of their conversation they shook hands and Commodore Madgwick said: "We'll make it happen."

So it was that the highlight of the 2007 programme, the Waterfront Gospel Festival, took place at the docks. The first day was a six-hour gospel concert in front of Liverpool's Maritime Museum; on the second was a massive service of repentance and celebration held on the deck of the Royal Navy Assault Vessel, HMS Albion, at Canada Dock. It was attended by the city fathers, many councillors, guests from other parts of the country and outside, including the Barbadian High Commissioner. An audio link was established with the Archbishop of West Africa so that he could contribute to the service from Ghana.

An extract from the ArtinLiverpool.com website[27], uploaded some days after the event, reads:

> City Sings Gospel, a project of Liverpool Lighthouse in the heart of Anfield, has spearheaded an incredible *Amazing Grace Festival* that has gone from strength to strength, supported by the Liverpool Culture Company, to mark the 200th anniversary of the abolition of the transatlantic slave trade and the 800th birthday of the city of Liverpool.

The Festival was launched at Liverpool Lighthouse in February with one of the North West's advanced screenings of Walden Media's *Amazing Grace*. The incredible line up of events has included numerous Sunday Night Live Concerts featuring local and international gospel artists, a live Sunday Morning Service broadcast on BBC Radio Four from the Maritime Museum and *Cargo* the musical. The highlight of the season of events was a magnificent Waterfront Gospel Music Festival that brought local and national artists together for a free gospel concert at the Albert Dock on Saturday 16th June including BBC Radio 1Xtra's DJ Fitz who was proud to be participating in such an event and a Transatlantic Memorial Service on board HMS Albion with dignitaries from across the globe on Sunday 17th June. Participants at the event included the Alabama State Senator Vivian Davis Figures, Bishop Errol Brooks, Bishop of North East Carribean [sic] and Aruba, Colin Hilton, Chief Executive of Liverpool City Council and Liverpool City Council Leader Warren Bradley, who described the event as a 'tremendously moving service.'

It was a significant event for the city, not only spiritually, but also in terms of giving us influence and favour with the city council. We were already known to them through our projects for young people, both Harmonize and our supported accommodation project, Bethel House. This festival, however, moved us to a different level of respect and recognition, which showed itself almost immediately.

Within a week or so three councillors approached us to find out if we would be willing to take over the trusteeship of a five-acre woodland park in a conservation area in Knotty Ash, to prevent it being sold to developers. The land had belonged to the Bright family, the city council taking over as trustee when they died out. The fate of the park had been in contention for many years; even the 'Squire of Knotty Ash' himself, Ken Dodd, had failed in his bid to acquire it to create a museum of comedy for Liverpool. This meeting was the start of the process that led to Liverpool Lighthouse becoming sole trustee of what we now call Bright Park.

Steve Chalke, in his book *Faithworks*[28], accurately describes the prejudice, hostility and suspicion with which Christian organisations, charities and initiatives are generally regarded by the statutory authorities, and the numerous instances of open discrimination they practise against such bodies (all in the name of religious tolerance).

As Steve states of his organisation's own experience when they approached a London borough council to talk about the possibility of working together to set up a 'foyer' for homeless people:

"...we had a real uphill struggle convincing some of the council's key players that we were both able and appropriate partners. A number of prominent council officials didn't like the fact that we were Christians, and they allowed that seriously to colour their initial judgements about our basic competence and suitability. Forget 'presumed innocent'. From the word go we had to mount a real defence against anti-Christian prejudice."

He goes on to say: "To their great credit, most of the council officials who had expressed either doubt or flat denial that it could or should be done have thrown their support behind us enthusiastically now that it's up and running. But I'll never forget the senior administrator who, after seeing the project video – made by the young people themselves...asked if he could have a copy for his own promotional use...but with all the 'Christian bits' cut out!"

Steve's book was published in 2001, and it would be idle to pretend that individual or collective attitudes have changed that much in the statutory world over the years. Even now, well into the 21st century, when economic pressures and lack of money have made councils more open to working with service providers of all sorts of backgrounds, the innate prejudice against faith organisations, and in particular Christian ones, runs very deep. Steve and his team at *Oasis* were not only able to prove that a Christian organisation could run a community project as competently and professionally as a secular one, they were able to demonstrate through their results that Christian organisations could achieve better outcomes because of the transformative impact of their God-given conviction that they transmit to those they reach out to – that every person matters.

That is what we too, by God's grace, had achieved in Liverpool. The following year, when we held a two-week International Festival of Gospel Music, climaxing in an open air festival right along Hope Street, with ten stages of gospel acts running from the Anglican Cathedral grounds to the steps of the Catholic Cathedral, the city fathers again attended. The Chief Executive joined Bishop James Jones and the Catholic Dean in a walk of peace along Hope Street, releasing doves at the mid-point and praying for the city. The *Liverpool Culture Company* underwrote the event to the tune of £50,000.

We realise that the body of Christ needs to build and maintain this kind of influence with the statutory authorities in every locality in the country. This is what gives us the opportunity to be prophet, priest and king to our cities and nations, and opens the way for us to influence every sphere of society for the kingdom.

After all, Christians have been instrumental in almost every civilising advance in society, whether in medicine and medical care, promotion of education, abolition of slavery, civil rights, emancipation of children, alleviation of poverty, promotion of social justice, even animal welfare. Whatever people may choose to believe, they cannot argue with the evidence. Current events – the financial crisis, the rise of poverty, the issues around migrants – give the body of Christ all sorts of opportunities to act, to speak up and re-establish its influence on society and its decision makers, not for worldly reasons but for God's purposes, seeking to support and work with the Josephs and Daniels that God has planted in strategic places.

Transformed to Transform

Chapter 14

LJM Association of Charities –
the Story Goes On
Hitherto has God brought us

At this time, Love and Joy Ministries Association of Charities consists of four registered organisations: Love and Joy Ministries Ltd, which we consider to be the spiritual parent of the Association; Liverpool Lighthouse Ltd, which is responsible for running Liverpool Lighthouse; Bright Park, the trust responsible for the five-acre woodland park in Knotty Ash, and Lighthouse Harmonize Education Trust, which runs our alternative provision free school, Harmonize Academy.

We use the analogy of a body to describe how the Association operates. Christ is the head, giving the instructions and direction. The Temple of Praise church congregation is the heart. The hands are all our community projects, and the feet represent mission and outreach.

Over the years from 2005 to 2013, through our Harmonize Project, we equipped over five hundred young people aged 13 – 19 who were excluded from mainstream education, at risk of exclusion or NEET[29], with GCSE equivalent qualifications and skills to move on successfully in life. From 2011 to 2013 we worked to transition the project to Harmonize Academy, a government-funded alternative provision free school specialising in urban arts and enterprise, and managed by Lighthouse Harmonize Education Trust. This school has now been running since April 2013. It was inspected by Ofsted in 2015 and graded Outstanding. We are now looking forward, by the grace of God, to opening other schools.

We have trained over 1400 adults, including asylum seekers and refugees, economic migrants, low-skilled adults and lone parents through our programmes of Basic Skills and ESOL.

Our Street Connect and Youth Connect programmes have engaged with more than 4000 young people on the streets and in the area, bringing them into positive activities, helping them make better choices in life, and also contributing to reduce the level of anti-social behaviour and petty crime in the area.

We have reached over 650 older folk, including 275 in sheltered homes, bringing them out of isolation and engaging them in arts, music and heritage activities that have improved their health and wellbeing.

Rose, now 70, who has been part of our older people's project for several years and is one of the beneficiaries who is also a volunteer, says: "Like a lot of the women in *Kaleidoscope* (the older people's project), I am a widow. Losing my husband five years ago was devastating. I lost my self-confidence and I felt so isolated until I found out about the Lighthouse. I made loads of friends and it's made my life worth living again. It is a lifeline for a lot of the community. People come every day just for support or advice; there is always someone who is willing to help."

Our volunteering programmes have helped many unemployed individuals into jobs. A large percentage of the staff who are now paid workers and managers started as volunteers. And we worked out that over a period of sixteen years, across all our projects we created approximately 350 jobs.

As an urban gospel arts centre we have trained over two dozen gospel choirs in schools, churches and community centres and run a number of major gospel music and arts festivals in the city. We have run gospel choir programmes with local schools and hosted world-famous artists and groups. Liverpool Lighthouse itself is a valued resource for the community, at various times hosting groups of adults with learning difficulty as well as other vulnerable groups and community activities, and offering affordable office space for new and emerging small businesses.

Within the last eighteen months we have embarked on a five-year project to work with disadvantaged families, bringing them together for fun activities and then equipping them with the skills to better manage themselves, their finances, their children, their physical health, and to support and befriend each other, family to family. Some of their comments indicate the impact of the project on their day-to-day lives:

"I have three children; I've never cooked a meal before, I only do microwave meals. I'm so happy I can cook now."

"Life is hard as a single mum; it's good to know someone cares."

"I was ill with stress, needing a lot of help to get away from loan sharks. Family Connect offered me one-to-one debt consultation and helped me out of that situation."

"We moved to Anfield two years ago; the project has allowed us to feel a great sense of community."

"Even training in the basic life-skill of cooking has made a tremendous difference," says Alfie, who has senior management oversight of the project. "One woman confirmed that as a result of the savings she made after attending one of our 'Cooking healthily on a budget' courses, the family was able to go away on their first holiday for years. Another learned to cook with us and became so hooked that she went on to do a higher level course at the local college."

Through Bethel Community Projects we accommodated about two hundred 16–18 year olds at a vulnerable period in their lives. In addition we provided move-on flatlets when they reached 18 years as an interim to them moving out into independent accommodation. How do we know that what we did had a lasting influence on their lives? We can be encouraged by people like Simon (again not his real name), one of the earlier residents of Bethel House, who came to visit Temple of Praise many years later, to tell us that he had gone on to become a qualified social worker himself, and was now seeking to help troubled young people in the way we had helped him. People like Mark, who, in spite of a serious wobble that could have destroyed him, was now settled, holding a steady job, with a family of his own, and would never forget what we had done for him.

We know that secular organisations could, to some extent, have provided at least some of the practical opportunities that we did. But, as David Evans commented, it was not the practical opportunities that spoke most to those whose lives were changed through our work – it was the presence of Christians living and loving, naturally sharing their lives with those among them[30].

And it is now, after so many years of sowing, that we are beginning to see larger numbers of people move from just participating in projects to coming to church meetings and making decisions for Christ. We have prayed for and reached out practically to our community for so long, and we look forward to the day when we will see full scale transformation in the lives around us, just as we can see physical transformation taking place through the regeneration of Liverpool Football Club and its environs.

****

As I write this, Temple of Praise is in its thirty seventh year as a church congregation. How many people have passed through the church? We don't know. From 2004, when we started to meet in Liverpool Lighthouse, we had the space to display flags for all the nations represented in the congregation, adding to these each time a new nation joined us. At present we have more than fifty, representing nations from every single continent. Of course, we have continued to suffer ebb and flow in numbers as young people have moved into Liverpool to go to university, joined the church, finished their studies and then moved away from the city in search of employment. This has been the case particularly with young doctors on rotation.

Nevertheless, we have covenant and/or daughter churches and ministries we support in Dublin, Leeds, London, Uganda, Kenya, Myanmar, Pakistan, Gambia and South Africa. This support includes some or all of finance, teaching and training, leadership development, mission trips and visits.

The transformational impact of LJMAoC in the region of Merseyside continues to attract interest from churches across England wishing to develop similar models of ministry. Temple of Praise continues to be an active member of *Together for the Harvest*, the local network of evangelical churches.

Tani continues as one of the directors of TFH, and in March 2016 became the first ethnic minority chair of the Evangelical Alliance UK in its 170-year history. During the year he also began the second three-year term as an ecumenical canon of Liverpool Anglican Cathedral.

To us, what we have been doing has been moved and made possible by five things. The first and most fundamental is the loving grace of God – his love and grace towards the lost and broken of Anfield and beyond, and his love and grace towards us that has enabled us to do whatever we have managed to do up to now, however imperfectly.

The second is obedience. God has only ever showed us one step at a time, and it is in looking back that we can see how taking each step opened up the next and then the next, each in its time. Not that we did not make mistakes – we did. The story I have told shows how difficult it was for us to cotton onto some things God was showing us that now seem perfectly obvious. I suppose what helped is that we never had any pre-conceptions about what God was going to do, so it was easier just to follow. How gracious of God not to have given us the whole picture at once – we would probably have taken to our heels, or died of fright! Or we would have rushed into things at the wrong time, things we were not yet ready for, and made a complete mess of them all.

Tani has been the main 'visioner' for the ministries, but he was surrounded by a group of early adopters. (After we finished the work on Liverpool Lighthouse, a group of early adopters informed him that the next time he had a vision for refurbishing an old building, they would lock him in a dark cupboard and leave him there!)

The third thing that God gave us was tools. When God had given Moses the mind-boggling instruction to go and lead his people out of slavery in Egypt, Moses (not unnaturally) raised the possibility that the people of Israel might not believe him or listen to him. God then asked him: "What is that in your hand?" The staff may have just looked like an ordinary piece of wood to Moses, but God used it supernaturally to convince his people, and to start the process of defeating Pharaoh. Looking back, we realise that there were a number of tools God put into our hands.

One was gospel music, and the choir. At the time we set up the choir, we did not know what doors it would open and the places it would take us to. Its loving family atmosphere, and the fact that it was mixed in nationality and skin colour, seemed to have an impact all of its own, especially as most other gospel choirs at the time were totally black. *Love and Joy* has sung the length and breadth of the country and at venues abroad. It has been the key 'act' at many prestigious civic events, featuring in the city's *European Capital of Culture* bid in 2003 and travelling with a group of councillors to Brussels to celebrate after winning.

Another tool was education. We went into teaching because the hours fitted in with raising children and building the church. We encouraged the young people who came to us to pursue education and training, and to aim to fulfil their potential. We did not know that in time we would open our own school. And we are still seeking God for the next steps, even as we begin to look to the future, and to those who will take the work on for the generations to come.

The fourth thing that has enabled this work is people. They range from those the Lord brought directly into the church, through those he brought in some capacity into the ministries, to the many whom God brought us together with through 'God incidences'. So many have been key to the development and work of the ministries. There are those who joined the church anything up to thirty years or more ago, and have stuck with it through thick and thin, going onto leadership positions within the ministry and organisations.

Others have moved away as part of God's plan, carrying the church's DNA, setting up ministries that are in covenant relationship with us or consider themselves daughter ministries, such as Living Grace in Dublin and Word of Grace in Leeds (led by John Adereti, who was one of our earliest deacons).

With many others we still feel a heart connection, even though separated by thousands of miles. We think of those who have supported us in different capacities, as friends and patrons of the ministries, including Bishop James

Jones, as mentioned earlier, Lord David Alton, Sir Mark Hedley, Lord and Lady Brentford, to name but a few.

And we deeply appreciate those that God brought to us through God-incidences, to encourage and input into us at specific stages, include Rev Rita Patrick of Dover, Delaware; Pastor Yemi Adedeji, now of RYA Consultancy. The list grows all the time. One of the most significant God-incidences was meeting John and Rose Lancaster, who through the support of their foundation have been generous beyond words. Without them LJMAoC would not exist.

The fifth ingredient is prayer, ongoing prayer. It is amazing that so many Christians run away from prayer, because, although it takes effort it is also one of the most essential and rewarding of Christian disciplines. Some of our most uplifting and enjoyable times have been spent in prayer meetings.

I remember particularly our overnight prayers and end-of-year fasting vigils, when the whole church would arrive with sleeping bags or quilts, supplies for the children, Bibles and writing materials, and settle down to spend two or three undisturbed days and nights with God. We worshipped, shared stories of God's goodness, studied the word, prayed, tested out our spiritual gifts – it was fantastic!

Tani and I had decided from the start to involve our children in whatever we did, so that they would not see ministry as something that took their parents away from them. As a consequence of this culture, children stayed with their parents during prayers and were encouraged to get involved. There was a separate room next door where they slept overnight, and played during the breaks. Many years later, those of that generation still refer to the fun they had together.

We even involved the children in fasting for a few hours a day during the vigils, once they were deemed old enough. Modern parents would probably throw their hands up in horror at the thought, but it is important to remember that at times in the Scriptures when God's people were called to fasting and prayer, especially in times of national crisis, everyone took part, regardless of age (for example, Joel 2v15-16, 2 Chronicles 20v 3-4, 13). It was also important that children should appreciate the value of food, given that there were, and still are, so many of their age perishing around the world from starvation. And in addition to building self-discipline and resilience in them, we were introducing them to the spiritual tools they would need to fight their own battles when the time came.

What we have come to recognise is that no local church is there by chance – each one is tasked by God to bring his kingdom to that locality (its own Jerusalem), using whatever God has placed in its hands. And from there God will move it to its own Judea and Samaria, and its own portion of the uttermost ends of the earth.

****

We have sometimes been asked how the ministry impacted on our family life, and the difference that it made. This can be somewhat difficult to answer, because in many ways our life and ministry were so closely intertwined. We obviously had to ensure that we gave the time to raise and nurture our children, and make them know they were deeply loved.

Right from the start we played with them, made up bedtime stories (Carrotman and Bananaman still feature in their memories), helped them with their studies, as well as tending to their physical needs. We connected a lot at mealtimes – we did not just sit round the table and eat, we discussed everything under the sun – current affairs, social issues, spiritual matters, fashion, news, education, the lot. People who dropped in to eat with us must have wondered if there was ever a time we were not debating something.

One additional feature of our lives is that we took on extra children. What was unusual about these ones is that they came to us as teenagers or young adults. In another context they would probably have been considered young 'uncles' and 'aunties' to our birth children, but because of the lack of parenting they had experienced as children, they sought parenting from us and were considered by our birth children as their older sisters and brothers.

One advantage of this is that it created an extended family circle that provided additional love and support for our girls as they grew up – other people to go to with their concerns. Since we were generally known in the church as 'Dad' and 'Mum', it was quite amusing to see the puzzled expressions on people's faces in public spaces when an obviously Caucasian man within fifteen years of Tani's age would call across to him: "Hey, Dad!" A consequence of our children's upbringing is that from a young age they gained the skills to interact confidently with people of a wide range of ages and backgrounds.

Tani and I are very different personalities. Because of his upbringing, he would have been happy to have 'open house' from morning till night, with people coming and going in and out of our home at will. I on the other hand, probably because of my upbringing, found the quietness and peace of the nuclear family unit to be a crucial sanctuary. For this reason, I instinctively played a greater part in protecting and hedging it about, creating a separate space where we could connect with each other and our children at the nuclear level, which to me also helped to maintain the stability of the family home.

I think one of the greatest blessings God gave us was a home built on love and laughter. Father Patrick Peyton, also known as The Rosary Priest, popularised the saying: "The family that prays together, stays together." That is true, and I also believe that the family that can laugh together, in the joy of the Lord, can face a lot of things together. Tani could always enjoy a good laugh. He liked fun TV programmes, even children's ones. I had a well-developed sense of the ridiculous. If a situation tickled me I sometimes laughed so much that I couldn't manage to get out a coherent explanation of what was so funny. The family would end up laughing at my laughter, rather than the joke. Our children grew up loving to laugh. Even today, when we get together, we discuss, and we laugh.

Transformed to Transform

Chapter 15

Facing the Challenges – Paying the Price

The cost of transformation

I remember attending a party at the house of one of the TFH leaders several years ago, and chatting to a young East African at the buffet table.

"Tell me about your church," he requested. As it happened, we had just been going through one of the particularly tough periods in the ministry. I mentioned a couple of our struggles to him.

"No," he said. "I don't want to hear about your struggles, I want to hear about your successes." I looked at him. "Our struggles are also our successes," I replied.

I don't know if my answer made any sense to him at the time. As Tani has commented, Christian leaders are always ready to talk about the great things that are happening in their churches; what they tend not to own up to are the difficulties and trials they have been or are still going through. Yet every ministry that succeeds, i.e., that fulfils its God-given mission, will face a whole range of challenges of different magnitudes at different times. Satan will not stand by smiling approvingly while God's people ravage his kingdom.

The most persistent challenge has always been finance. As will be common to much of Christian ministry, we never started with the money to undertake any major step God instructed us to.

"At the time we were facing a £1 million plus project, the church's annual turnover was around £30,000," says Mike, the treasurer.

Tani and I had already sunk any personal savings we had into the ministry, and there were several others who also gave every penny they had to spare, and frequently money they couldn't really spare. One might wonder why the One who owns the cattle on a thousand hills could not just provide the needed cash in bulk so we could focus on getting the work done. We could also wonder (I certainly did) why he allowed so much money to remain in the hands of the ungodly, when we could put it to so much better use! But we sowed – through fundraising activities, funding applications, giving, pledges and labour, and God blessed our efforts, making them fruitful and also granting us some generous benefactors. We had to step out in faith, and then he provided.

Even now it is all too easy for people (including church members) to walk into the building and assume that because it is large and functioning, it must be prosperous, and that there is no need to give. The truth is that without the generous, ongoing commitment of the whole congregation, the work of a transformational church will always struggle.

Next to finance were the people challenges and these have taken many forms. There is surely no congregation that has not suffered what a visitor from Scandinavia described as 'shakings', when a persuasive individual with an agenda would foment a rebellion and eventually lead a walkout. As Tani's brother put it, every church contains the good (the stable), the bad (the unstable) and the ugly (the destabilisers). Every now and again the destabilisers would rise up to do what they were there for. These situations were always stressful and deeply unpleasant, but we found that God, having cleared them out, would then bring in others who were more committed, with even greater gifts and skills, people who considered it an honour to serve in the ministry. Each time we ended up looking back and thinking: "Why did we worry?" The only grief was over the weak ones who got led astray.

Transience had its impact on the ministry. The relatively poor economic situation in the Northwest in general, and in Liverpool in particular, meant that there were not always suitable graduate positions available. Consequently we developed so many sound, committed young adults in Christian ministry only for them to move elsewhere when their studies were over. For instance, in one year we welcomed a group of 30 performing arts students who came together from LIPA (Liverpool Institute for Performing Arts). They got stuck into the choir, worship, drama and music teams, bringing their own particular energy, liveliness and skills; then they all graduated and left together, leaving us to rebuild yet again. Added to this now is the busyness of people's lives: shift patterns, weekend working, lengthening commutes, childcare pressures. The focus and discipline required to serve become incomprehensible to those whose primary understanding of church is as a body that exists to meet their needs.

Numerical growth likewise has had its own consequences. As the church grew larger it became more difficult to maintain the close-knit, family dynamic that it had enjoyed for so many years. Longstanding ties were being stretched by the need to look after others. We even found when we started to worship in Liverpool Lighthouse, which we did from 2004, that the very structure of the auditorium, though great for services, made mixing more difficult. It was easier to overlook people, and it was also easier for people to hide, or cluster with their familiars. We have had to constantly look for ways to encourage interaction, to promote positive relationships, and to develop small groups around discipleship, ministry, and fellowship.

Another impact of numerical growth showed itself over time. When we were still at the stage where all the church members had become believers through the ministry of Temple of Praise, it was easy for everyone to subscribe to the same set of values, and for these values to be reinforced in a natural way through the strong family relationship. As the church expanded it attracted other believers who loved being part of Temple of Praise but had different views on matters that were important to us.

A case in point was alcohol. Pentecostals by tradition do not drink. In our ministry there was an additional impetus for a 'no alcohol' policy. We ministered to so many people, old and young, whose lives had been ruined by it in one way or the other – how could we fellowship with them and yet indulge in the very substance that had brought them so much grief?

Not all the church members took such a view and this sent mixed messages to the newer and weaker believers, some of whom now found excuses to continue embracing habits that were unhelpful at the best and destructive at worst. And it was not just alcohol. There were other Christian disciplines we took for granted, such as tithing, communal fasting and prayer, that others did not seem to consider important or necessary. Again, we found we needed to be patient and persistent in teaching and encouraging folk in these areas.

A constant challenge in a multinational church like ours is maintaining a balance in composition. Africans and Caribbeans have a church-going tradition which the type of populace in our local community does not. Moreover, human beings are generally attracted to those who look like themselves. We therefore have to work and pray hard to ensure that Temple of Praise remains 'a house of prayer for all nations'. The need for balance extends to spiritual and socio-economic composition. It is not possible to build a thriving church consisting exclusively of broken, needy people. There have to be enough strong ones to minister to and support the weak; enough mature Christians to develop and encourage younger believers.

Likewise there have to be enough wage earners to give financially at levels that allow the church to run. The Lord Jesus came to preach good news to the poor, but his followers included wealthy women who provided for him out of their own means. TOP's congregation ranges from those with higher degrees to those with no qualifications at all, from professional earners to those on benefits. The ages range from babes in arms to senior folk in their 80s and 90s. Again we have to ensure we are meeting the needs of this range of members and attenders in an effective way.

An ongoing struggle is bringing the people in the church along with us on the path of community transformation. This was the case during the development of Liverpool Lighthouse, and we are still working on it. Many people come to church to be looked after; making them see our projects as part of the church's activity has not been easy. For those involved both in the church and in the projects, there has of course been no problem. But perhaps for the very reason that we are immersed on a day-to-day basis in the wider ministry's business, we can forget how far removed some of it seems to those who come into the building only on Sunday.

So we have to strive to keep the congregation informed, encourage them to volunteer and create a sense of ownership. We also look for opportunities like open days and special celebrations to bring the church and those involved in projects together. The obstacles are not all on the church side – we have to encourage non-Christian staff to do things on an occasional Sunday without making them feel pressurised.

Last but not least, there is the critical issue of succession planning. Life is long, but a period of thirty or more years can pass so quickly that suddenly the pioneers find that they are ageing and that others need to be in place and ready to carry on the work when they are gone. There is also the issue of ensuring the legacy and making sure that others can learn from our experience.

And what about the price? When the Lord Jesus said to his first disciples: "Come, follow me," I do not know if they realised that their lives were going to change in every way, forever. At the time the Lord called us to this ministry, on that 24th of September 1979, we were just building careers as chemical engineers, were settled members of a local church, and had been married just over nine months. Within a few short years of that call, our time in industry was completely behind us and we had diverged into a totally different path. No doubt, had we continued as before, we would have retired by now on respectable company pensions. Instead, we moved into a world of engagement with communities that we never knew existed, and began to deal with people whose paths would never otherwise have crossed ours.

Tani had been a Christian since his teens, but I had been a Christian just over two years, so for me it was a complete move out of any sort of comfort zone. We were not even planting out of our existing local church, so it was a completely pioneering venture. At times we seemed to be climbing with no 'handrails' to hold on to, and no prior example to follow. The newness of it all could be pretty scary.

One area where there was no stinting was that of sheer hard work, whether that was the physical labour involved in refurbishing our buildings, or the hard work of ministering to people and managing as well as governing organisations and projects. I first became pregnant around the end of 1979, so was expecting for most of the period that we travelled into Liverpool three of four evenings a week after work.

That, however, was a doddle compared to working on the central heating system in Durning Road while pregnant with my second daughter. There were two of us expecting at the time (we eventually had our babies within a day of each other), but this second pregnancy was particularly sickly. I felt nauseated throughout the first five and a half months, and by the time that phase passed I was getting too bulky to bend and kneel easily. Moreover the smell of dust and sweat at the building site didn't help matters. That period certainly counts as one of the most physically and emotionally demanding in my life.

To be truthful, everyone who was committed to the ministry paid the price. I already mentioned the price in terms of money. (Very early on we had decided that we would stick to a 'tent-making' ministry, so that the word of God could be preached freely, without fear or favour.)

Apart from hard physical work, we also laboured in that essential discipline without which nothing could have happened – prayer. We prayed in our homes, with prayer doublets, in whole church meetings, overnight vigils, three-day fasting prayers, forty-day Lent fasts, the lot. The ministry was birthed and built in prayer, and without it would fall apart. Even our children paid the price, because they were always with us. They enjoyed the blessings of the close fellowship, but they too were affected by the blows we experienced.

Paul wrote in his letter to Timothy that *'everyone who wants to live a godly life in Christ Jesus will be persecuted'* (2 Timothy 3v12). While discrimination and social pressure are still more common in this country than out-and-out persecution, we have experienced troubles, including once being arrested for something we knew absolutely nothing about. Another time, a contractor fell while working in the building's roof space and subsequently died. It is only now, seven years later, that the matter is coming to an end. And among the voices questioning whether we had sinned, were those declaring: "You must be doing something right, if the enemy is getting so angry."

What can we say? Ministry is a marathon, not a sprint. It is about serving. And we press on, seeking always to discern the Lord's will, looking forward to the day when we hear him say: *"Well done, good and faithful servant...Come and share your master's happiness!"*

Appendix

Chapter	Ref/ Note No	Item
4	1	https://liverpool.gov.uk/council/key-statistics-and-data/ward-profiles/
5	2	https://www.theguardian.com/cities/2015/sep/14/toxteth-riots-1981-summer-liverpool-burned-patrick-minford-jimi-jagne
7	3	http://www.revival-library.org/index.php/catalogues-menu/1904/evan-roberts-revivalist
7	4	https://www.theguardian.com/cities/datablog/gallery/2014/jul/03/where-atheists-live-maps-uk-godless-cities-religion-census-data-viz
7	5	*Black Liverpool - The early history of Britain's Oldest Black Community 1730-1918*, Ray Costello, Picton Press, 2001
7	6	Ibid, p12
7	7	Ibid, p 13
7	8	Ibid, p 14
7	9	Ibid, p 17
7	10	Ibid, p 18
7	11	Ibid, p 55
7	12	Ibid, p 57

7	13	Ibid, p 58
8	14	*The rise and fall of Liverpool sectarianism. An investigation into the decline of sectarian antagonism on Merseyside*, Keith Daniel Roberts. Thesis submitted in accordance with the requirements of the University of Liverpool, Department of Politics, for the degree of Doctor of Philosophy. April 2015.
8	15	Neal, F. (1988) *Sectarian Violence: The Liverpool Experience 1819 – 1914*. Liverpool: Newsham Press – p.158, as quoted in Ref 14, p 1
8	16	Waller, P.J. (1981) *Democracy & Sectarianism: A Political and Social History of Liverpool 1868-1939. Liverpool: Liverpool University Press* – p.xvii, as quoted in Ref 14, p 4
8	17	Ref 14, p 251
8	18	BBC (2008*) Statue for two Bishops*. Available: http://www.bbc.co.uk/liverpool/content/articles/2008/05/12/faith_bishop_statue_feature.shtml - The pair were dubbed 'fish and chips' 'as they were always together and never out of the papers'. As quoted in Ref 14, p 251.
8	19	Interview with Reverend John Williams – 17th November 2010, as quoted in Ref 14, p251
8	20	Ref 14, p251
8	21	Longley, C. (2000) *The Worlock Archive*. London: Geoffrey Chapman – p.314, as quoted in Ref 14, p251

Appendix

8	22	A week-long Christian youth initiative taking place in August 2005, in partnership with Merseyside Police, involving non-stop clean-ups in some of the most under-privileged suburbs, and culminating in a weekend festival in Croxteth Park. Merseyfest drew 25,000 people daily. See, for example, https://www.christiantoday.com/article/uk.larges t.christian.youth.initiative.merseyfest.a.huge.suc cess/3777.htm
9	23	The Christ Apostolic Church was founded in Nigeria/Ghana in the 1950s by Joseph Ayo Babalola. It has autonomous establishments in many countries across the world.
12	24	*Creating space for strangers – Thinking afresh about mission and the church*, David Evans with Kathryn Scherer, Inter-Varsity Press, 2004
12	25	The Single Regeneration Budget (SRB) was set up in 1994 to bring together a variety of programmes and initiatives from several Government departments. The aim was to simplify the funding process and to provide resources to support regeneration initiatives carried out by local regeneration partnerships
13	26	A TV and radio producer, recognised as a pioneer in promoting British Gospel Music.
13	27	www.artinliverpool.com/city-sings-gospel-sunday-july-15-07/

13	28	*Faithworks – Actions speak louder than words*, Steve Chalke, Kingsway Publications, 2001
14	29	Not in education, employment or training
14	30	*Creating space for strangers – Thinking afresh about mission and the church*, David Evans with Kathryn Scherer, Inter-Varsity Press, 2004, p 57, 58